Don Lyons was born and raised in Peoria, Illinois. He is the third child of seven. He graduated from Manual High School located in Peoria, Illinois. Later in life, Don attended Illinois Central College and obtained his associate degree in special education. He then transferred to Bradley University in Peoria.

Don worked for the local school district in Peoria as a special education teacher assistant while pursuing his teacher credentials. Don retired after 16 years of faithful service to his students. Don has adopted five children, and during his 25 years as a foster parent, he fostered over 100 children.

This book is dedicated to my loving wife who allowed me the time to write.
It is also dedicated to my "muse" Elise and to the greatest teacher, Miss Sharon Crews.

Don Lyons

MY NAME MADE
A DIFFERENCE

AUSTIN MACAULEY PUBLISHERS™
LONDON • CAMBRIDGE • NEW YORK • SHARJAH

Ordering Information
Quantity sales: Special discounts are available on quantity purchases by corporations, associations, and others. For details, contact the publisher at the address below.

Publisher's Cataloging-in-Publication data
Lyons, Don
My Name Made a Difference

ISBN 9781643785882 (Paperback)
ISBN 9781643783949 (Hardback)
ISBN 9781643784182 (ePub e-book)

Library of Congress Control Number: 2020922993

www.austinmacauley.com/us

First Published (2021)
Austin Macauley Publishers LLC
40 Wall Street, 33rd Floor, Suite 3302
New York, NY 10005
USA

mail-usa@austinmacauley.com
+1 (646) 5125767

I would like to take the time to say thank you to Austin Macauley for being there for me. Also, thanks to my family for encouragement and belief in me.

Chapter One

Hello, my name is Blythe Taylor. I am a nineteen-year-old senior from Rolland High School, and graduation is less than two months away. I'm excited for two reasons. First, out of two hundred students in my graduation class, I ranked tenth. Secondly, I have applied and been accepted into Winston State University in the fall. It is my plan to study to become a teacher.

Although I'm excited about my future, my past had proven to become very difficult – difficult because of bullying at school. Bullying impacted my life so greatly to the point of my not caring about school, my grades, cheerleading, or life in general.

During my fifth and sixth-grade year at Rolland Middle School, I tried out for the junior varsity cheerleading squad, only to be turned down in each one of them. I was discouraged but talking to my mom always made me feel better. I decided that there was always next year, so I channeled all my frustrations into working harder. I worked hard practicing my clean position, my clap position, and the High-V position. I gave extra attention to this position by making sure my fists were tight, and they looked like donut holes. Then I practiced the last two positions, The Low-V and the T-Motion positions. Cheerleading was important but not as important as keeping up my grades, so first thing after school I would complete my homework and then practice my positions until dinnertime. I was determined to make the Varsity squad my seventh-grade year.

Chapter Two

The summer passed of my sixth-grade year. It seemed like an eternity. Maybe it was my anticipation of working hard all summer on the positions, or I had a gut feeling that I would finally make the squad. In any case, my seventh-grade year had finally arrived. Cheerleading tryouts were held immediately after school began. We had to be ready for football season. There would be three cuts in all. Then there would be the final list. It was simple as this. If your name made it to the final list, you made the squad.

My name made it through all three cuts in two days. After the final tryout on the third day, I checked the list. Finally! There was my name in black and white, Blythe Taylor. I wanted to yell and scream, but I kept my composure. At that moment, I realized that I had persevered to become a cheerleader. In hindsight, I used the same tenacity from my studies and applied it to cheerleading.

So, I had accomplished two successful things in my early school career, and I was elated. Everything was finally going as I planned. However, as hard as I had worked to maintain good grades, perfect attendance, and now making the squad, things would soon start to become dismantled. At that point, I would have worked even harder to maintain my sanity.

Chapter Three
Family Life

I told Mom that I made the squad. We hugged each other, and she let out a loud 'yes.' I began to show her some of the positions which I practiced all summer. I was so happy, and I guess all the restrained happiness which I kept bottled up from before, I let it out at home. I think my mom was even more excited than me.

My parents were not my biological parents. I was adopted at the age of five. The last time I saw my biological parents was when I was five and we were all at the termination of rights and adoption hearing.

My caseworker, Miss Jensen, told me a few weeks before the hearings what would eventually take place. She told me that eventually Mr. and Mrs. Taylor would become my permanent parents. I guess I should have cried and screamed. However, the Taylors had been very good to me. They were the only real parents I knew. My biological mom and dad made me promises that we would be a family again, but it never happened. As a matter of fact, if I can remember, they only made two visits successfully. As far as my siblings were concerned, I had a younger biological brother whom I'd seen only once. Miss Jensen told me he was adopted by another family in another town.

I made up my mind that despite everything, the Taylors were my parents – end of story. Mom and Dad had one other child named Alyssa, and she was two years younger than me. However, our relationship was very good.

We weren't only sisters; we were great friends.

In my secret thoughts, I wondered what it would be like to have known my biological sibling, and he and I would be very close. I would also like to know who all my biological family was – people like aunts, uncles, cousins, and who my paternal and maternal grandparents were. However, one thing blew my mind. During dinner, Dad and Mom asked me if I were happy with being together with them. I replied, "Of course." I asked them why they asked that.

Dad replied, "Well, it must be tough having to call people who your biological relatives' family are not, so Mom and I discussed this issue together and we both agreed to ask you that question."

I was about ten years old and very able to ask and answer questions. I told them that they were the only family I knew, and they had loved, provided, and cared for me up to this point. I also said that I couldn't have asked for better parents and sister. The last thing I said on this subject was that I loved all my relatives no matter what.

This was the first and only time this subject came up as a family. However, my private thoughts were my own. I knew I was satisfied because there was never any desire for me to bond with anyone else than my family. My name was Blythe Taylor and that was final.

As Alyssa and I got older, we didn't hang out as much as we used to. We always remained loving toward each other, but with me now at sixteen and her at fourteen, we each had our own friends. We made a vow to always keep our sisterly bond. We accomplished this by keeping our lines of communication open. We could talk about anything from boys to anything that might be troubling to one of us. Although I was set to enter college and leave home soon, we still had that bond intact.

Chapter Four
The Hard Times

Life was going smoothly for me. My grades were good. I was a seventh-grader, and now I was a varsity cheerleader. Life was good. I was pretty much of a loner at school because I was focused on keeping my grades up; and that meant studying hard at school and at home with my parents. I didn't have much time for anything else, oh, except for spending time with my sister.

But despite all these wonderful things, I still felt inadequate in some things. First, I never wanted to discuss my being adopted. Secondly, I never felt pretty enough to fit in. I stood at 5'4" tall. I had short black hair and brown eyes. I also had freckles, which I yet maintain to this very day. It seemed like the older I became, the more the freckles spread. Although I disliked the freckles in my earlier years, I had come to realize that beauty comes from within first. I couldn't hide the freckles because of my very light skin tone.

At first, no one just came out and said anything negative to me. These were just my fears, but soon my worst fears would be manifested into reality. Cara was a girl who also tried out and made the squad. Unlike me, she made the squad in her previous two years. Cara was nice and pleasant to talk to. I had seen her at the tryouts and even in the halls, but for some reason, we never connected. However, this year was different for some reason. Cara and I became inseparable at school and sometimes after school. She told me that when she was in fifth grade, her parents went through a divorce.

She said she was very sad and unhappy at one time because of the divorce, but she still spent time with both her parents. She lived with her mom, but her dad got her on weekends. She got to spend more time with him during the summer.

Cara and I contrasted with each other in some ways. For instance, I was 5'4" tall. Cara was a few inches taller than me. I had black hair. Cara was a brunette. I was from bi-racial parents, which gave me a light skin color. In any case though, Cara and I just loved and appreciated each other for who we were. We never talked about our family situations. I guess it never mattered. Despite our physical differences, we had a lot in common. We both loved pizza, chocolate shakes, and cheerleading.

It was now the middle of October, and the school year was progressing greatly. Everything was going swimmingly. Then we had a new seventh-grade student named Lindsey Brecker. She was an only child and said her father was transferred here by the engineering company he worked for in California. Lindsey stood about 5'7" with long, blond, flowing hair. I must admit she was a beautiful girl on the outside, but later her indifferent personality made her less becoming and attractive.

Lindsey decided that she desired to be a cheerleader, so she approached Morgan, the varsity captain, that she wanted a special tryout because it would be unfair to not have one. Morgan tried to explain to Lindsey that tryouts and the final picks had already been held a month previously, but Lindsey was insistent that she was a cheerleader at her school in California, and she would love to have that opportunity here.

Cara and I listened to the exchange between the two, and Morgan agreed to her request for a special tryout at today's practice after school. Cara and I didn't say a word. We just looked at each other and smiled. That look meant we could tell that Lindsey was used to getting her way, and she wasn't about to take 'no' for an answer.

Later, at practice, and before it began, Morgan introduced Lindsey to the squad and that she was giving her a special tryout. Lindsey was given ten minutes to show what abilities she possessed, and she was very good at front and back flips and roundhouses. Her talent impressed the judging panel and the rest of the squad so greatly. We all accepted and welcomed her to the squad. After practice, Cara and I went to introduce ourselves and congratulate Lindsey in becoming a part of us.

Lindsey looked us both up and down and had this seemingly look of superiority on her face. Her face no longer showed that bright smile that was portrayed earlier in the day. I said to her, "My name is Blythe Taylor."

Cara attempted to introduce herself, but Lindsey cut her off. "Blythe, what kind of name is Blythe? Is it German or something?" I never gave my name's meaning a thought. It was just a name my parents gave me, like all parents do. I couldn't answer her question because I was dumbfounded that she would ask such a question upon our first meeting – or for any meeting.

Finally, Cara said, "My name is Cara."

Lindsey replied, "Well, at least your name sounds more American than hers. Well, I'm off, girls. So glad we had this little chat. See you later, girls."

Cara and I were stunned. We looked at each other, and this time there were no smiles. That expression, "A picture is worth a thousand words," goes very well here. At that moment, words were beyond us, and for a moment, all we could do was stare at each other. Finally, Cara spoke, "Do you believe her? The nerve of her. Who does she think she is?"

I replied, "It takes all kinds, I guess. Come on, let's go get a slice of pizza and a shake."

As the time passed, the insults grew worse, and Lindsey's words became harsher. To this day, I have no idea what started her verbally attacking me. She made comments about my freckles by saying things like someone could pass the time by playing connect-the-dots on my face. On one occasion in the cafeteria, Cara and I were sitting together, as we usually did, when Lindsey told some kids seated at another table, "Hey, you boys want to rent out her face for a dollar to play connect-the-dots?" The boys looked at me and laughed uncontrollably. I felt humiliated. Cara and I sat at this very table every day across from the same boys and never had any problems until she came.

There were days when she would talk about my weight. Yes, I was short, but I was far from fat or heavy. She made comments like I would give the other cheerleaders a hernia when they would try to lift me, or why my butt was so huge. She would say anything to get a laugh at my expense. I couldn't believe that this was my third year at this school, and I never had any problems. Now, Lindsey has gotten nearly everyone turned against me. Where I used to walk the halls with no problems, now it seemed like everyone was pointing and jeering at me. Looking back in retrospect, it wasn't true. I was just imagining these things because of how I felt inside. All of this was due to the hurtful things being said. I tried to ignore the comments, thinking they would stop or just go away. However, just when I thought they had ended, it became even worse. I came into gym class, and there was a picture with my name. The picture was of a girl with freckles like mine. It showed the girl with a bloated stomach and behind. The caption was in big letters, saying, *"FRECKLE-FACE, YOU HAVE NO PLACE!"* Kids were laughing hysterically. I took the picture to Mr. Lee, the P.E. teacher. He simply dismissed it as a prank. I didn't see it in the same vein as he did. I was humiliated and hurt to the point where tears welled up in my eyes.

I yelled out between sobs, "This is not a prank!" I had never cried in front of anyone because I never had a reason to. I didn't even cry when I found out the Taylors weren't my biological parents because they always took great care of me. This day, I cried, and the more I cried, the more the kids laughed.

I wonder how one girl could cause such an uproar. Cara and I had the same gym class, and she saw the picture as well. Gym class was the last period, so school would be out for the day. Cara tried her best to make me feel better by saying we could go get a pizza and a shake. I was too upset, and I guessed Cara noticed a different expression on my face, and she must have concluded in her own mind that this wasn't a pizza-and-shake moment. Thankfully, there was no practice that day.

I was hurt on the inside. It seemed that all I had worked so hard for had seemingly come to naught. Cheerleading, which I loved, didn't matter to me anymore. At this point, even my grades or school didn't matter anymore. After arriving at home, my mom met me as she usually did. However, my face must have been showing what my heart was feeling – broken and in pieces. I tried desperately to hide my pain, but evidently to no avail; it didn't work.

Mom noticed that I wasn't my jubilant self because on a normal day, I would've headed straight to the refrigerator for a cold drink and a snack (if I weren't out with Cara after practice). Now I felt too miserable to eat. Mom asked me, "What's wrong?" I didn't want to upset her, so I played it off by saying I was only tired. She looked at me longingly as if she didn't believe me, but only smiled and said, "Okay." I told her that I was going to my room and lie down until dinner. I went to my room and decided to text Cara. I didn't want my mom to hear us talking about today's incident. I was telling Cara to keep the incident to herself, hoping it would all soon blow over, but knowing deep down inside that I was only being untrue to myself.

Cara texted me back immediately. Our texting seemed simultaneous. Her words brought shock and terror to my heart. She said there was a message on social media, and it said that there was a foster/adopted child named Blythe Taylor who attended Rolland Middle School. It went on to say, "Evidently, her real parents didn't want her. We don't want any foster kids in our school."

Immediately, tears welled up in my eyes. I started crying hysterically. My heart sank. Cara tried texting some comforting words, but I could hardly make them out because of the torrent of tears. Soon, Mom was knocking on the door and vehemently shouting my name, "Blythe! Blythe, what's going on? Blythe! Please let me in." I hesitated because I was numb and seemingly frozen in the bed. Slowly, I began to come to myself. I remember Mom yet screaming for me to let her in. I thought, 'What am I going to tell her? What will I say?' I felt so embarrassed. However, in retrospect, what did I have to be embarrassed about?

I guess mentally I was trying to make sense of all this and come up with a logical explanation for my mom. It seemed like an eternity for these events to take place, and for me to come to reason. I weakly called out and asked Mom to give me a second. I needed to regain some form of composure. It seemed like I was moving in slow motion to get out of bed. Yet, my mind was racing to regain my thoughts.

I opened the door to my mom's panicked face. She was wiping tears from her face and eyes. She asked me what was going on, and what made me so upset? All I could do was hand her my phone and show her the text from Cara. Immediately, she grabbed and hugged me. I felt safe and secure at that very moment. I didn't want her to let me go. "I'm so sorry, baby," she said. "Who did this?" she asked. I told her it was from an unknown source, and it came from someone on social media who I didn't know. Mom asked me if I had been having any other problems at school.

That was when I began to tell her the whole story from the beginning to the end. I told her all my troubles began when Lindsey came to school and became a cheerleader and how she immediately started talking about me.

"Honey, why didn't you come and talk to me?"

"I thought I could handle it, Mom. Plus, I thought it would go away. Now, because of this thing on social media and what happened earlier today—"

Mom interrupted, "Just what happened today?"

"Well, Lindsey, I guess she passed this note in gym class that read: *'Freckle-face, you have no place.'* That's why I came in the house and not my usual self." I went on to tell her that I hated my name. I hated school. I hated the name Blythe, and I hated Lindsey.

"Sweetheart," Mom stated, "I can clearly see that all of this must be upsetting to you because I've never heard you talk in this manner. I wish you had come to me and let me know what was happening from the beginning. I want you to know that I love you very much, and your father, your sister, and I are here for you."

"I love you all too, Mom," I replied. "Mom, I know that I'm not your real family but —"

Mom interrupted, "Stop that right now, young lady. You are our family, and more so. Let me tell you something I learned a long time ago. When two people decide to have a baby, they don't get a choice of what baby they get. They must love and accept the child they get. You, on the other hand... we made choice of you, and that's what makes you special to us. We love your freckles and everything else

23

about you. Furthermore, I looked up your name's meaning, and it means carefree. That's what we want for you, to be carefree and with no worries."

Instantly, I began to feel better, and I said, "So, that's what my name means? I guess I never really thought about it." Mom and I continued our conversation, with her reassuring me that everything was going to be fine and my confidence slowly returning with each word from her.

Looking back now, my mom has always been there for me. I understand that she wouldn't be able to fix every problem that would confront me. However, this one experience with Lindsey really taught me how to handle myself in adversity.

The next day, both families had a meeting with the principal. First, we met separately, and we went first. I told the principal what happened each day, while my parents listened. When I finished, he told us to have a seat in the waiting room while he talked to the other family. I was not sure exactly what he said to Lindsey or her parents, but when we were all assembled in his office, he announced that Lindsey was responsible both for the note in gym class and the post on social media. Although the post wasn't under her name, it was easily traced back to her cellphone.

Lindsey was informed that these were serious matters and were expulsion offenses. He went on to say that she had apologized to him and her parents, and now she must publicly apologize to me. She had to use the P.A. system the next morning to publicly apologize for her hateful acts. There were two other conditions that she would have to meet. First, she had to resign from the cheerleading squad for the rest of the year. Secondly, she had to undergo anger-management training with the school's social worker. The next morning, she did as she promised by apologizing after the announcements on the P.A. system. I felt happy that this was all behind us now. As a matter of fact, Lindsey, Cara, my sister, and I now go hang out at the mall and even go get our favorite, a slice of pizza and a chocolate shake.

To some, the things I went through probably wouldn't add up to be anything but a molehill, but to a seventh-grader, things of this nature can be devastating. After all, some children in the seventh grade find themselves in an awkward place. For one, we were no longer in the sixth grade. Secondly, we weren't in the eighth grade, which meant that we were still two grades away from high school. This made some of us feel out of place. Now, on a personal level, I not only had to strive hard to maintain good grades, try out several times for the cheerleading squad – only to be successful on my third try – I had to now undergo this traumatic experience of having my personal and family business placed on social media.

I attempted to act like these events didn't bother me, but for some reason, I couldn't hide my true feelings from my mom, so she talked to my dad and they agreed to get me a mentor. I met her on a Saturday. Her name is Linda Espinoza. We had fun times, just the two of us together in the beginning. Then later, we would invite Cara to come with us. Linda shared with me that she was a victim of bullying as well, and how she overcame it. She shared that her family moved to the United States from Mexico and the difficulties she and her family had in adjusting to American culture. She was teased because of the clothes she wore, the color of her skin, and her lack of not being able to speak

English. She also said that it seemed the harder she worked to fit in, the harder some children made it for her. She remembered some of the girls calling her derogatory names such as 'Wetback' and saying, "Mexicans are lazy and dirty." She shared that many times she went home crying to her parents. Her parents met with the teacher and principal. They agreed to investigate it, but her parents never heard anything. She said this continued until her ESL teacher intervened on her behalf. ESL stands for English Speaking Language. This teacher worked diligently with Linda on learning English and, with her parents' permission, bought clothing and bathing items for her. Linda said she really began to feel good about herself. She said that she had enough self-esteem, to the point that it didn't matter what anyone said about her. She said she became a mentor because she wanted to return the same favor her ESL teacher did for her.

Linda worked with me the rest of the seventh grade. I guess she wanted to make sure that I would be okay. First, we were meeting twice a week, then down to once a week, and finally down to once a month. By the time I reached the eighth grade, I didn't hear from her except for an occasional text. Linda already knew that I had supportive parents, and she was a temporary addition in my life, someone I could identify with, and I did.

It was the summer after graduation from high school. Cara and I were trying to spend as much time together as possible before it would be time to go off to college. Alyssa and I remained close as sisters, but she developed a relationship with her own friends. My little sister was a sophomore in high school. As for Cara and me, we vowed we would see each other when we returned home at the end of each semester, and we would text, call, and *FaceTime* each other when time permitted. Cara decided to go on to a local junior college and then transfer to a four-year college.

Lindsey told me that she wouldn't be able to attend graduation because her father's job was being moved elsewhere immediately. It was said that they didn't even have a chance to sell their home. Yet, there was a 'for-sale' sign in front of their home before their leaving. Lindsey confessed to me that this wasn't the first time she had to suddenly pack up and move. This explained Lindsey's previous negative behavior toward me. She didn't have any real friends, nor did she know how to make any real friends.

I could now see that she was empty inside. I began to feel sorry for her. Her parents gave her any materialistic thing they could, but nothing makes up for spending time with your family and friends. For a moment, I thought how blessed I truly was. Although, I had no relationship to this day with my biological parents or my sibling, God blessed me with wonderful parents and sister. They didn't just give me things. They surrounded me with love. They were there when I needed them most in the seventh grade.

Cara and I spent the summer preparing for college. We went shopping for clothes, but we still on occasion went for our favorite, a slice of pizza and a chocolate shake. It was getting close to dinnertime, so we had to quickly scarf down our pizza and shake. When we were finished, we said our goodbyes. When I got home, I quickly washed my hands and sat in my usual place at the table.

Mom and Dad were both smiling like the cat that ate the canary, and seemingly just as excited because Mom couldn't stay seated. I looked at Alyssa, and she looked at me, both of us with puzzled looks. Just then, Mom blurted out, "Girls, we are going on an all-expense paid cruise for the four of us!" She went on to explain that Dad was given this opportunity at work. We had been on family vacations before, but never a cruise. Now Alyssa and I were smiling as well. Dad said we must get packed because we were leaving in two days. Suddenly, reality struck. 'I must break the news to Cara. How will she take it? I will be gone for only five days, but will she be okay with it? I miss her already.'

With these thoughts in mind, I asked my parents if I could be excused. They said I hadn't eaten anything. I told them that Cara and I had pizza and a chocolate shake earlier, and I wasn't hungry. I didn't lie. I just held back what was going through my mind. I didn't want my parents to worry or mess up their exciting news. I called Cara when I got to my room. She quickly answered on the first ring. Her voice was excited and upbeat as usual when she answered. "Hello," she said. "Blythe, I'm so excited about us both going to college in a little while, and I loved the outfits we picked out today."

I interrupted, "Cara, I have something to tell you, and I don't know how to tell you."

"Blythe, just say it. It can't be that bad."

I took a deep breath and let out the words with the same breath. "Our entire family is going on an all-expense-paid cruise vacation for five days." There was a momentary pause on her end. I think she might have been waiting for me to say something else. During that momentary pause, I felt as if I was breaking the only real friendship I ever had. That pause seemed like an eternity.

Finally, Cara said, "Girl, is that all? I thought you were going to say something earth-shattering like someone was sick or something. I understand completely, so go and have yourself a great time."

The summer of our graduation was hurriedly ending. I had less than two weeks before I would be off to college. I went into what seemed like a trance of all that had happened and was happening. I briefly reflected about the bullying incidents in the seventh grade and how I got through them with the help of my family, my mentor, and my BFF Cara. Then, I suddenly thought, 'Cara… I'm going away from my best friend for three months.' It all began to hit me. No more slices of pizza and a chocolate shake for a while. I began to reflect on how much fun we had during those times. I thought about how hard I persevered to maintain good grades and make the cheerleading squad.

'I'm on my way to college,' I thought to myself. Despite all my setbacks, I was truly on my way. I made a solemn vow to myself that I would do as Linda did for me – to invest my time in someone that has the same or greater problems.

The two weeks went by very quickly. Winston State was a four-hour one-way drive. Cara was there alongside my family and me on my departure day. Dad loaded all my things in our SUV while Cara and I hugged each other and said our goodbyes. I promised myself that I wasn't going to cry when the day finally came. However, that promise quickly flew out the window the moment we hugged. We both realized that we would see each other in three months. However, when you have a friend that is just like your sister, and you have spent most of your time with this person, three months' separation is like an eternity. Yet embracing each other, tears welled up in both our eyes.

We promised to text, call, and chat whenever time permitted. We released each other on the sound of my dad's voice resonating, "Time to go, Blythe." I had high excitement and expectations of leaving for school, but I must admit that leaving all I was accustomed to was very difficult. Alyssa and I got in first and then Mom and Dad got in the front seats. It was very hot and humid outside, so Dad quickly turned on the air conditioner. As I looked up, I saw Cara mounting her bike and waving goodbye. Tears were in her eyes and her eyes were bloodshot red from heavy crying. With tears in my eyes, I pressed both my hands against the window. Cara came over and matched my hands on the glass. Dad had turned around to see if it was clear of any oncoming cars, and he gave us a moment. He slowly backed out of the driveway as Cara released her hands from the window. As he put the car in drive, I turned around to see Cara. She put in her ear buds and peddled away.

Chapter Five
College Life

The closer we got to the university, the more nervous I became. I needed some reassurance, so I asked Mom a question. "Mom, do you believe that I can make it? I mean, do you feel like I really have what it takes?"

Mom replied, "Blythe, it's not important what I believe, honey. It's what you believe. I will say this. Look at all the obstacles you've overcome in your life and look at what you've had to endure, and now look. You've finished high school and you are less than an hour away from enrolling in college. I think that's phenomenal, isn't it?"

Alyssa chimed in, "Sis, I'm going to miss you, and I love you and I think you'll do greatly." I didn't expect any reaction from Dad because he really didn't like to talk and drive. But in this case, he also reiterated Alyssa's words of expression. I said, "I love you all as well, and I know that I couldn't have made any of this possible without my family. You guys have been my rock and I thank God every night for parents and a sister like you. I will make you all proud of me."

At the conclusion of these words, Dad was pulling into the parking lot of the registrar's office. I had to go there first, to get my class schedule and dorm assignment. There were a litany of cars and people outside, and I suppose inside as well. We all got out of the car and went inside. Everything was just as I said. It seemed like thousands of people filled that tiny room.

We entered one of the long lines to be waited on. Alyssa went and sat down to wait, but Mom and Dad stayed with me. When it was finally my turn, the lady said with a smile, "What's your full name?"

I replied, "Blythe Marie Taylor."

She asked for the spelling of my first name, and I told her. "Blythe," she said. "I've never heard of a name like that, but it's cute and original. What does it mean?"

"It means carefree," I replied.

While she was talking to me, her finger was going down a list of names. "Blythe M. Taylor, it says here you completed a campus visit last year. Is this true?"

I replied, "Yes, ma'am." She handed me several papers while explaining each one. One paper would give me access to my dorm room, and the other I was to take over to the campus police to get my I.D. She told me that their office was closed for the day and to go the next day. I asked her about class schedules. She said I had two choices to obtain my class schedule. I could either return to the registrar's office tomorrow or I could get it from their website that was on the bottom of I.D. paper. I said 'thank you' and left for my dorm room.

I remembered where the dorm was from my earlier visit. I think Dad forgot, and I directed him. He acted like he knew all along where he was going. Upon our arrival at the dorm, we all pitched in, gathering all my things from the car. I grabbed my laptop first thing to make sure I had it because it would become a great part of my life this semester. Alyssa spotted an unused cart – for transporting items – and we loaded my clothes, shoes, and other items.

Once everything was loaded on the cart, we proceeded toward the front entrance. Right above the front glass double doors was a sign in big black and red letters, *WILLIAM'S HALL*. Those were also the school colors. I pulled out the dorm assignment paper and it had the numbers 5543 in red letters, and next to it were instructions that this would be the access code to the dorm entrance, and it was also my room number. As we are all crowded around the entrance, I entered the number and pushed the button. Immediately, the opened as we made our way to the elevators, for the fifth floor. The elevator stopped on the fifth floor and we scrambled to get off. 'The elevator is going to get a lot of work today,' I thought to myself, and that became true because as soon as the doors closed, you could hear it moving immediately.

It was only a short distance to my room, but it seemed like an eternity to get there, seeing we had to push through a great crowd of people and their possessions to get there. Finally, I was standing in front of 5543. I quickly inserted the key into the lock and opened the door, and at that moment, someone came from behind. I turned and looked and saw the biggest smile I had ever seen. It was followed by a very warm, yet very excited, greeting. "Hi, I'm Mandy, and you are?"

"My name is Blythe Taylor. This is my mom and dad and my sister, Alyssa."

"Nice to meet all of you. Blythe, can I help you unload any of your things?"

"No, my family and I have everything covered, I think."

At that same time, my parents and my sister were bringing in the things from the cart, and my dad said, "Everything is out of the car, honey," as he laid the last box on the empty bed. The one other bed already had boxes and a laptop computer on it, so I assumed it belonged to Mandy.

It was 5:30 p.m. The time really had gone by. My dad said, "Blythe, honey, it's getting late. Let's all go out for a bite to eat."

I interjected, "May Mandy come too?"

Dad gave a quick, puzzled look at Mom. In return, she gave a quick nod of her head, which meant an unequivocal 'yes.'

"Yes, honey, Mandy too. After dinner, I will bring the two of you back to the dorm so you may finish unpacking your things. The three of us have a reservation at local hotel. Tomorrow, we will then check in to see how everything is going with you at that time, okay?"

"Yes, sir," Mandy and I said simultaneously while smiling.

Dinner took about two hours, and Dad did just as he previously said. He dropped us off and told me to finish my unpacking, and he would see me tomorrow. Mandy and I exited the car and approached the dorm building. Dad slowly pulled away as I turned to wave goodbye. I knew we would see each other tomorrow, but this would be my first time away from home, and the first time away from my family. I missed my family already, and despite the excitement of being in college and being on my own, for a moment I felt sad inside, and I was like in a trance. I quickly shook off the melancholic feelings because I could hear Mandy calling me, "Blythe, Blythe, what's wrong?"

I murmured back, "Nothing. I was just thinking about my family. I'm all right, so let's go unpack and get to know each other, since we're stuck with each other for the next three months or so."

"Great minds think alike, so let's go," Mandy said.

When we got to our room, the farthest we achieved in unpacking and getting our room in order was making our beds and putting a few of our clothes away. We both acted as if we were too exhausted to continue, so we just stretched out across our beds and began to talk. After all, the two of us were going to share this room together, so it was essential to know each other. However, how do we begin this talk? I didn't want to come across as being nosey or seem to be the prying type. While lying on the bed trying to come up with the right words, Mandy just came out and asked, "Where did the name Blythe come from? I mean, I've never heard it before, and I'm not making fun of it either." I was relieved and stunned all at the same time, relieved because I didn't have to make the first move and stunned to think how she dared ask me about my name.

I responded, "My name means carefree, but there's a long story that goes along with it."

"We have nothing but time," Mandy replied.

I began telling her that I was adopted at the age of five years old and that I met my parents only once that I can truly remember, and that was at their rights' termination hearing. "What is that?" Mandy replied.

"It's when your biological parents appear before a judge in court and say they will no longer make any decisions nor have any parental authority over you. Then, those rights had been transferred over to my adoptive parents. The Taylors are the only parents I've ever really known, and they have taken very good care of me.

For example, my parents are footing the bill for my college education."

Mandy said, "You're lucky. I'm here on financial assistance. My mom and dad divorced when I turned fifteen. Dad left us with very little money to live on. My mom worked hard, and I had to take care of my two little brothers. Somehow, I managed to maintain good grades. Maybe it was because I saw what my mom was going through, and I made up my mind to work hard like her. I was picked on in school because I didn't have the fashionable clothes or shoes. The kids in school nicknamed me 'plain Jane full of shame,' but I'm here now at Winston State University. I'm going to make something of myself, and I'll show them. I will show them all. They will all be sorry for messing with me. I will show my dad too. Who needs him?"

"Sounds like you have a lot of anger," I replied.

"Well, wouldn't you if you'd been through what I've gone through?" replied Mandy.

"No, I wouldn't, and no I won't."

"Wait, what do you mean you won't?" cried Mandy.

"I won't because I forgave everyone who hurt me. I forgave my parents for giving me up. That must have been a blessing in disguise because look where we are today. It doesn't matter if you're here on financial aid or anything else. The fact is you made it. I was bullied in middle school because of the freckles on my face, how short I was, my name, and that I was an adopted child. This new girl even put my adoption business on social media in a derogatory manner to hurt me. I wanted to give up. I wanted to quit. I had worked hard to make the cheerleading squad and to maintain good grades, but this girl, without provocation, wanted to hurt me. I hated school and I hated the teachers for not protecting me.

"It wasn't until my mom told me what my name meant, and she was right there for support. I forgave the girl because I found out that she really didn't have any real friends nor the time to make any because her father's job moved her family from place to place. I also forgave her because life is too short to hold onto grudges."

By this time, we had both sat up on our beds. We sat silent and still. Tears had welled up in my eyes. Mandy's head was bowed, and I could only see her face partially. I wasn't sure what her action would be. I thought to myself that she might say that she thought she was better than me or even want to change rooms. It was at that moment while her head was still bowed that a great big tear dropped onto her bed. This was followed by several other tears. Mandy broke the silence by saying, "Looks like we both have things in common. There is one thing for sure. Life is too short to hold onto negative things. Blythe, you have really taught me something tonight, and I'm going to be different from now on. I won't feel sorry for myself any longer and I must let go of the past." We hugged each other while a few more tears fell from both our eyes. Mandy then said, "Okay, enough of all this mushy stuff. We must get some rest because tomorrow we both have a lot to get done."

Then I replied, "You're right." We both said goodnight. I lay in bed and reminisced about today's events. I was happy that Mandy and I were roommates, and hopefully as the time passed, we would draw close as friends.

The next morning, I was awakened to running water coming from the bathroom. I glanced over to Mandy's bed and it was empty. Then I looked at the clock on my phone and it read 6:30 a.m. Lazily, I sat up on my bed, and at the same time I heard the shower go off. A few seconds later, Mandy peeped her head out of the bathroom, displayed a smile, and said, "Morning, roomie."

"Why are you up so early?" I grunted but smiled also.

"I always get up early. My mom always taught us it's the early bird that gets the worm. I'm not going after any worms, but I have a lot on my agenda to get done today, and after last night's talk, I'm ready to take on the world. So, what do you say, roomie? Are you ready to get out of that bed and get started?"

I replied, "I'm as ready as I'll ever be. Let's start with breakfast because I'm starved."

"Okay, sounds good to me," Mandy replied. After showering and getting dressed, we headed for the cafeteria downstairs. We hurriedly gulped down our breakfast which consisted of scrambled eggs, bacon, toast, and coffee. On our agenda was to obtain our I.D., then come back to finish putting away our things, downloading and printing out our class schedules, and reach in time for lunch. It was now 8:30 a.m. We looked at the I.D. paper which said the security office would open at the same time. As we got close to the office, my phone suddenly rang. It was my dad. "Hello, Dad."

"Good morning, Blythe. Did you sleep well?"

"Yes, I did. Thanks for asking. How are Mom and Alyssa?" I asked.

Dad replied, "Everyone is fine, but listen, we are heading downstairs to breakfast. Then we plan to head over to see you. Let's say around ten o'clock, okay?"

"That sounds fine, Dad. Mandy and I are on our way over to the security office to get our picture taken and get our I.D."

"Okay, sounds great. See you soon."

"Bye, Dad," I said.

Mandy and I both had our papers in hand as we entered the campus security office. We stepped into a small, brightly lit room where stood a young African-American man dressed in a grayish uniform with red trim on his shirt and a red stripe-down on each pants' leg. He looked very official with his shiny silver badge.

"May I help you?" he asked in a very calm tone. Mandy and I looked at each other when suddenly she gave her head a quick nod. I knew from that she wanted me to be the spokesman. "Yes, sir, we have come for our I.D." We both handed the officer our papers, and he quickly glanced at them.

"Okay, you are both freshmen." We both nodded our heads in agreement. He looked at both of us with a huge smile and said, "Welcome to Winston State University. It will take only a moment to get your pictures, and only a few moments more to print out your I.D. Then you can be on your way. Now, who wants to go first?"

Since I was more relaxed since he smiled, I spoke out, "I will go first, sir." He asked me to step over to this area where a computer and a camera were. He took my paper with him and gave Mandy to hold onto hers until he called her. He told me to have a seat in front of the camera, but he began to type my information into the computer. It seemed like he had done this a lot because he finished typing very quickly. He then instructed me to look straight into the camera with just a straight face. "You're finished. It will take a moment for your card to come out. Please ask your friend to come get hers." I left the desk and summoned Mandy that it was her turn. Within moments, Mandy too came out to me. The officer soon followed her. He handed us our cards with that same huge smile. "Here you are, ladies, and once have a great day." Mandy politely said 'thank you' while I nodded my head in agreement.

The last thing on the agenda for the day was to print out our class schedules. Since we were close to the university library, we made a choice to print them out on their computer. After going inside, we came upon a tall semi-circled desk where two young people and an older lady with grayish hair and dark rimmed glasses sat behind. The two young people smiled at us, but the older lady did not smile. "May I help you?" the older lady abruptly asked.

I quickly spoke up before Mandy, "Yes, we need to print out our class schedules."

"You may use any of the desktops, or you may use your school I.D. to check out a laptop to use in the library only. Do you have your I.D.?"

We both replied, "Yes, ma'am."

"Excellent, so which will it be, ladies?" Mandy and I looked at each other. We had become so close in so short of time; we could almost know what the other one was thinking. Without saying a word, we both simultaneously handed the lady our I.D.s. She looked at both our I.D.s very closely and then looked very carefully at Mandy and me. After a few moments, she reached directly behind her and pulled out two laptops in a case. "I'm sorry for taking so long and being hesitant in looking at your I.D.s, but last year we lost three laptops due to people passing off as our college students with fake I.D.s. The university was having students that wanted to rent the laptops to provide a credit or debit card to hold it. However, they rescinded that just at the beginning of this school year."

As she took our I.D.s, she said, "This laptop can only be used within the confines of the library. It must be returned before the library closes at nine p.m. Once you are finished, you return it here and your I.D. will be returned to you. Do you understand?"

"Yes, ma'am," we replied.

I began to draw a negative conclusion about this woman. I wanted to think how she dared talk to me as if I were a child. Who does she think she is? Instead, I thought that the woman was only doing her job, and I remembered what my name meant, and that was 'carefree.' I said to myself, 'When adverse situations come against me, I will remember what my name means.'

Mandy and I took our laptops over to some very huge, comfortable chairs. Logging into the system was easy because I had already set up my username and password at the orientation. However, I wasn't certain of Mandy. "Mandy, have you set up your username and password?"

Mandy replied, "Yes, I did it during the orientation. We had not met then. There, I'm logged in."

"Me too," I replied. Soon after that, we found our schedules in the form of the four-page syllabus. We eagerly sent them to the library printer.

Arriving at the printer, we found out there was a cost of ten cents per copy. I told Mandy, "No, sweet, this is my treat." I used my cash card to pay for the copies. A cash card was a lot like a credit card, and it could be used for practically anything. A person may also use it to purchase their books, purchase food and clothing, plus any other expenses. My mom and dad thought it was a great idea because it would be much easier to load money onto my card from home than to send a check in the mail or to wire money. The only drawback the card had was its limitation to purchase things off-campus. There were only a few restaurants located off-campus that accepted the cash card.

Chapter Six
Classes Begin

Classes began on 22nd August, and now the real test would come in the form of my classes and assignments. I felt I was ready in the beginning, but as the time drew closer, I wasn't so sure. I would bounce some of my emotions off Mandy, and I felt that she was growing weary of my emotional rollercoaster. However, she would always listen to me and reassure me that everything would be all right.

My first class began at eight o'clock a.m., and I was awakened by the noise of the shower. I glanced over at the clock and it read six-thirty. Rubbing my eyes to see if I was seeing the correct time, I lay back down and covered my face with my hands. Then a few moments later, I heard the shower go off and Mandy opened the bathroom door while a huge, billowy cloud of steam escaped into the air. "Why are you up so early?" I asked.

"Well, good morning to you too, Miss Grumpy. We both have an eight o'clock class and we can't be late on our first day."

"I guess not. I really must come to terms with college life, in that so much more is expected of you in college."

"So, come on and get up, sleepy head, and crawl out of that bed. We must get breakfast and get ready for the day," Mandy said with this huge, bright smile.

All transfer students must do their general education studies first. If I stayed on the course outlined by my advisor, I would have my general education studies completed within the first two and a half years. Once they would be completed, I must apply to the Teacher Education Board for my three-hundred-level courses, which included my novice teaching and student teaching. I realized then that this wouldn't be an easy task, but anything worth having is worth fighting for. Also, I knew that it would be difficult four years at times, but if my name really stood for what it stood, I will succeed. I was pondering all these things to myself as I showered and Mandy and I headed out our dorm door. "Mandy, it's great to be here," I said. Mandy simply showed that bright smile and nodded her head in agreement.

After breakfast, Mandy and I went our separate ways for classes. I was headed to Lewis Hall for my psychology-110 class. I had this class on Monday and Wednesday from eight to ten a.m. Then I had my philosophy-110 class from 10:30 to 12:30 on Tuesday and Thursday. Friday was my 'math for teachers' class from three to five p.m. This course simply taught the different ways to teach math to students, and since I was going into special education, this class would come in handy.

I quickly arrived at Lewis Hall. I pulled out my schedule to check on the room number and the professor's name. The room number was 132, and the professor's name was Professor Moore. I walked a few feet after I entered the outside glass door. I guess I must have entered the building at the proper point because just a few more feet in front of me, I could see the proper number and name. Lewis Hall was four stories high and there was no way to get lost because the entire building was in a circle.

I was ten minutes early, so I took a seat in the front, since the back row was occupied. A few more people trickled in after me, but with about two minutes before eight o'clock, all the seats were filled. Immediately after the seats were filled, a young, athletic-looking young man entered. He looked to be over six feet tall with dark hair and dark eyes which seemed to look right through me. I'm sitting in my seat mystified because I was expecting, for some unknown reason, a short, bald old man. His voice rang out and I quickly snapped back to reality. "My name is Professor Moore as it states on the syllabus. Welcome to psychology-110. I trust everyone brought their syllabus with them because it is my practice on the first day to get acquainted with one another and go over the assignments for the semester and answer any questions," he stated.

He had each one of us to stand, state our name, and tell a like and dislike of ours. When it was my turn, I said, "My name is Blythe Taylor. I love reading, and I dislike children being bullied." The room was silent, and the professor had a look of concern on his face as well. He had started from the back of the room, so I was the last to speak.

His expression quickly changed as he spoke, "Thank you all. These exercises will help us all to get to know one another better this semester, and the reason being, you will be assigned to groups for projects to do." While he continued to go over the syllabus, I continued eyeing the cute professor. I don't know why I hadn't noticed it before. Maybe I was blinded by his good looks, but there was a big shiny, gold wedding ring on his left ring finger. I quickly paid more attention to what he was saying and was no longer focusing on his good looks. He allowed us to leave early, since there was nothing else on the agenda. I took this opportunity to sit under a big shaded tree and read a book until my next class. Since it was the first day, my next two classes pretty much followed the same procedure as the first class. Each one of the professors allowed us to leave early after going over the syllabus. There was one thing they all stressed about the assignment deadlines though. They all said that there was a hard-and-fast rule on turning every assignment in on its due date, and the grade would be lowered each day it was late. Mr. Davis, my philosophy professor, said that he had heard every excuse known to man as to why a particular assignment has been tardy, from 'the dog ate it' to 'a family member suddenly became ill,' and they were the only ones who could sit by their bedside in recovery.

Sometimes, we forget that our professors are people too, and they probably attempted some of the same excuses we try to use. I made up my mind that each one of my assignments would be in the digital drop box on the designated day before midnight, so I devised a plan. The digital drop box was on the school's website. Once you logged into the drop box, you had to choose your professor's name from the list, click on the assignment, and upload into his or her box. My plan was to work for at least fifteen minutes on each assignment that was nearest to having to be turned in. I would spend as much time as I could between classes to read, do research on required papers, and work on assignments.

I would work hard Monday through Friday, but Saturday would be my rest day, but with college life, one never knows what will present itself. I arrived back in my dorm room at 5:15 and Mandy was lying across her bed with her ear buds in her ears. Although she had them in her ears, I could almost hear what she was listening to. "Mandy." There was no response. "Mandy!" I shouted.

Mandy looked up surprisingly. "Hey, Blythe, why are you shouting?"

"I'm shout– oh, never mind. How was your first day, Mandy?"

"It was good. We didn't have very much to cover other than the syllabus in each class."

"That sounds like the same as me," I replied. "I need to call my parents and let them know how my first day went. Then if you're hungry, I feel like treating us to a pizza at DE Vecchio's Pizza Palace."

"I'm famished," Mandy shrieked. I lay on my bed and relaxed while I called my parents. I dialed the number and after three rings, a sweet voice came on the other end of the line.

"Hello, Blythe. How are you, sweetie? How was your first day?" Mom's voice reminded me of old times. It yet settled me and caused me to relax, such as learning that my parents never wanted me, having a biological brother whom I don't have a relationship with, or a girl in middle school who blasted all of my family information all over social media.

"I'm fine, Mom, and the first day went well. We only covered the syllabus today in each of my classes." Although, I had made up my plan to succeed this semester, suddenly out of nowhere came a sense of uncertainty. This unsure feeling must have resonated in my voice because Mom began to encourage me. Some might call it 'mother's intuition,' but whatever one might call it, I was so glad my mother had it.

"Blythe, honey, I want you to know how much we love and miss you here. Just one thing though. As you progress, things tend to get a little more difficult. If you're not careful, assignments can overwhelm you to the point where they will stress you out. I'm not saying these things to scare you but instead, to help prepare you. You are a brilliant young lady, and I know you will succeed at anything you put your mind to. Just remember how you fought to make the cheerleading squad, and you finally made it. Then, when Allyson bullied you and you thought to give up on cheerleading, your grades, and possible life itself, you fought back like a champ." Tears began to well up in my eyes and roll heavily down my cheeks. I attempted to say something to Mom, but my voice was quivering. I took a long sigh.

"M–mom, college is all new to me. I had mentally put together a plan for myself to succeed, but in the recesses of my mind, the thought of not being good enough comes—"

Mom interrupted, "You are good enough. It doesn't matter what took place in the past; it's what you do now that counts. Despite all you have been through, God must have told your mom to name you Blythe. Sometimes He chooses

48

the plain things in life to confound the wise, and that is precisely what He has done for you, honey."

"Thanks, Mom. I will make you and Dad proud. Tell my little sister I send my love, and I love you all."

"We love you too, honey. Goodbye."

While wiping the tears from face with my hands, I took a deep breath and said, "Mandy, are you ready for some pizza?"

Mandy replied, "Are you okay? And yes, I'm ready if you are. What happened today? What did your mom say?"

"Everything is fine, and my mom was just saying some things. We can talk about it over pizza, okay?"

"Sounds great to me," replied Mandy.

DE Vecchio Pizza Palace was about a ten-minute walk from our dorm. It was surrounded by several other fast-food restaurants on a brightly lit thoroughfare. To look at the place, one would wonder why the owner would have the audacity to call this a palace. It was anything but that. When I used to read fairytales as a kid, I visualized a palace with a lot of brightly lit rooms, beautiful tapestry on the floors and walls, and a décor to die for. This place was just the opposite, with its dimly lit rooms, linoleum floors, and plain chairs and tables. The pizza was great.

We ordered a large half and half pizza and two soft drinks. Mandy wanted only pepperoni as her meat topping, and I wanted sausage. I swiped my card when the total bill came up. The cashier handed me the receipt, two large plastic cups, and the Number Thirteen on a small sign. The cashier informed us our pizza would be brought out to the table in fifteen minutes. We carried our cups over to the soda dispensary, filled our cups, and then took a seat. "So,

Blythe, spill it. What's going on with you?" she asked as she took a sip of her soda. Mandy must have realized my hesitancy. "Blythe, we are friends, and there I want you to know that there is nothing you can't confess to me."

"Mandy, there are times when I feel unsure of myself. I have a great family that supports me with much love, and they have been there when my biological family wanted nothing to do with me. Sometimes, this all feels too good to be true, like I'm dreaming and will soon wake up and the dream will be over. I am blessed, and I know it, but sometimes…"

"Blythe, you are lucky, and I would trade places with you in a hot second. I watched how carefully your family made sure you had everything you needed when they dropped you off, and even stayed overnight to say goodbye the next day. My family was barely able to get me here. I am in college on a part-academic scholarship and part-financial aid. I had to work hard in high school to maintain good grades despite being picked on because I couldn't afford the clothes that some others thought I should be wearing."

"Wait, you were bullied?"

"Yes, I was bullied because of my clothing and shoes. Many of the kids were wearing fashionable shoes, but we couldn't afford the same clothes and shoes. I am the oldest of four children, and my mom is single. My dad passed away two years ago from cancer." Heavy tears began to hit the tabletop from Mandy's eyes. She lowered her head so as not to be noticed by others as to what was going on. I handed her a napkin to clean herself while she struggled to regain her composure. "Blythe, I can remember a time when our water was disconnected because we couldn't pay the bill on the due date. I heard my mother pleading for an extension for the next day because that's when we would receive our paycheck.

"She pleaded that she had four children and we needed water. My mother tried to hide her sorrow from us. I made sure she couldn't see me, but I could see and hear her. My mother was a tower of strength, and I never saw her cry before that day, but I will never forget that look of pain and sorrow that I witnessed on that day. I got a part-time job while I was in high school to help out, and I made up my mind to work hard and make something of myself."

"Wow!" I interjected. "My mom said on several occasions that when one complains about what he or she is going through, there is always someone going through worse situations. I'm sitting here feeling sorry for myself. Mandy, you have never shown any of this, and I'm sorry."

"Don't be sorry," said Mandy. "I'm used to it, and I will be fine."

"Mandy, if you need anything…"

"I'm no one's charity case."

"I didn't mean it that way," I said. "I know you will be fine. I'm looking at how we ended up together as roommates, coming from similar backgrounds. I couldn't have asked for a better roommate, and I hope we become the best of friends."

"Blythe, I would like that too. Oh, Blythe, I forgot to tell you that I played soccer in high school, and I'm trying out for the team here."

"That's wonderful news, Mandy. Here comes our pizza. Are you ready to dig in because I am famished?"

"Let's dig in, Blythe," Mandy said.

The events of this evening turned out to be phenomenal. Mandy and I drew closer, not just as roommates but we connected as true friends. I could see what my mom had been telling me all along, that my name was identical with my character. It didn't mean that I would never have any encounters. My name meant that despite any circumstances which may present themselves, I was not to be worried or distressed. God knew exactly what to name me. We continued with our evening with fun and laughter. Although the room was crowded, the two of us were oblivious to who or what surrounded us. We enjoyed each other's company. I began to reflect briefly on mine and Cara's relationship back home. It seemed like I always had that one good friend just to be there. I made up my mind to not be so self-absorbed with my inadequacies, not that I will ever forget my own emotions but not allow them to overtake me to the point where I forget the needs of others. I learned that these self-pity moments can easily sneak up on you if you're not careful. I didn't know what the future held for me, but I would face it one day at a time. I won't try to speculate for tomorrow, for I could hear my mother's voice saying, "Don't worry about tomorrow because there is enough to do today." We had remaining of the pizza one piece each, and we were both full. I asked for one carry-out box to take the remaining pizza back to our room and we departed.

When we arrived at our dorm room, it was about seven o'clock p.m. Since we had such a wonderful time at the pizza place and we talked while we walked home, we were both talked out. Mandy took no time in stretching out on her bed with her ear buds in her ears. I figured that tomorrow's classes would probably follow the same format as today's classes. However, I wasn't taking a chance on that. It would just be my luck that tomorrow's philosophy professor will want the reading done. I took my philosophy syllabus from my notebook, and sure enough it said there will be a class discussion from our reading Chapter One. I took out my blue-and-white-covered philosophy book titled, *The Awareness of your Subconscious,* flipped through Chapter One, and saw it was only eight pages in length. I was glad that tomorrow's class was later in the morning, but it would be easy to complete my reading tonight after I took a shower. I gathered my towel and headed for the bathroom. While in the shower, I began to reflect on today's events. What really blew my mind was how I was able to listen to Mandy when she was supposed to listen to me. I guessed that was how things worked sometimes in life. I said a silent prayer, thanking God for all He had done for me. I thanked Him for my family, the opportunity of being in college, and for a great friendship with Mandy. It had to be God that strategically placed people in my life who encouraged and helped me through the bullying incidents. After showering, I quickly put on my pajamas, grabbed my textbook, and hopped into bed. Carefully, I began to read the assigned pages. By this time, Mandy arose from her bed and went into the bathroom. Shortly after, I heard the shower come on, and I resumed my reading. By the time I reached Page Four, I didn't remember anything after that because I fell into a deep sleep.

The Next Day

Morning seemingly came in a hurry. I was awakened to a bright, narrow beam of light peering through a crack in the curtain, shining right into my eyes. From then on, I would make sure the curtains were completely closed. I rubbed my eyes and turned to look at the clock. It read 6:30 a.m. I could hear a stir in the bathroom. After a few moments, the bathroom door opened, releasing a huge, billowing cloud of steam. "Good morning, roomie," came this voice out of the midst of the cloud of steam.

Still half asleep, "Morning, Mandy," I mumbled. "What time is your class?" I asked. "I have an early class at 8:00. What time is yours?"

"I have class today from 10:30 until 12:30."

"Are you going down for breakfast?" Mandy asked.

"I'm probably only going to have coffee. I am still full of last night's pizza. Plus, I have to finish my reading for class today."

"Well, come on, let's get a move on. I hate eating alone." I scurried out of bed, quickly showered and dressed, and then out the door we went. The cafeteria was filled with students and cafeteria workers. The cafeteria workers were busy replacing the empty pans in the buffet lines. They had a buffet filled with sausages, scrambled eggs, and bacon. Then there were stations where one could make their own waffles. All one had to do was take and fill a small cup from the batter container, pour it into the waffle maker, and turn the waffle iron over. In about three minutes, the waffles were done. There was a buffet with fresh watermelon, cantaloupe, honeydew melons, and various other fruits.

Lastly, there was a station consisting of a cereal variety. Mandy went to the scrambled-egg section and I went straight for coffee. When we were satisfied with our choices, we sat down. "You know what, Mandy? I wish we could have a car on campus." The rule was only juniors and above could have personal automobiles on campus.

"That would really be nice. Then we could really have some fun," she said with a mischievous grin and a wink. "I'm only kidding," Mandy said.

"I know, I was thinking how nice it would be to be able to go to the mall without having to take the campus trolley or the bus. Oh, well, that time will be here before we know it," she said, glancing at the wall clock, "and speaking of time getting here quickly, it's 7:45. You better get going." Mandy got up from her seat and hurriedly gulped down the last bit of her breakfast. Her mouth was so full that she couldn't verbally say goodbye, so we just waved at each other.

I headed upstairs with the remainder of the coffee in the cup. Once I reached my room, I took my book from the bed and sat down at the desk and began to read. I didn't dare lie on the bed for fear of going back to sleep and being late for class. Nine-thirty soon came. I had finished my philosophy reading by 8:30, so I started reading my psychology textbook for tomorrow's class.

I remembered my vow to try and stay one step ahead in my assignments. After refreshing myself, I took my textbook, laptop, and my cellphone to the lounge area on our floor. There were a few other girls in the lounge as well. Other than the few of us, this floor, which was normally very hectic, was presently a ghost town. After playing a few hands of online solitaire, I took out my philosophy syllabus. It stated that our first paper would be due in two weeks. It also stated for us to not begin on the paper until the professor gave us the directions. I left for class at 10:15 and headed for class. It was only about a five-minute walk, but I wanted to give myself plenty of time.

Arriving a few minutes before the required time, I noticed that the teacher, like my other class, wasn't yet present. Unlike my other class, the room was nearly full, with only three seats in the middle of the room. I quickly took my seat. I found myself thinking what Professor Roberts would look like. I visualized that he was just as good-looking as my first professor. A few moments later, a gray-haired elderly woman walked into the classroom. With expectations that she would fill into one of the remaining empty seats, to my shock, she assumed the teacher's desk in the front. I laughed within myself for being wrong again.

"Good morning, class. My name is Professor Sharon Roberts, and welcome to philosophy-110.
I have a little ice breaker that I use to help us get acquainted. I would like for everyone to stand and form a circle around the classroom. Then I want the first person to state his or her name and one like you have. Then the person next to you will say their name and their like, then say the person's name and like. Then the third person will have to say their name and their like, then say the two former person's name and like, and so forth and so on."

The two people on my left went first, and both did it seemingly with ease. When my turn came, I stated my name and my like. I did for both people without any difficulty. However, subsequently, there were two times when a few people had difficulty in reciting a person's name and like. In those cases, we simply laughed while the class would help the struggling person.

After the exercise, we regained our seats. Professor Roberts brought up the syllabus on the smart board. "There are two things I have planned. I want to go over the assignments listed on the syllabus and the due. Secondly, I want to go over today's reading assignment. As you can see, there are four papers due throughout the course of this semester, and each paper counts as a major part of your grade.

"Each paper must be in APA style with a work-cited page. There is a due date for every assignment, and they must be in my digital drop box before midnight of the assigned day. The assignment is considered tardy if it dropped one second after midnight unless you have prior permission from me. For each day the assignment is late, the grade will be lowered by a letter grade.

"There will be three major tests, not including your midterm and your final exam, and pop quizzes. Each test will cover the reading of three chapters. Are there any questions?" No one raised their hand or answered. It seemed like everything was self-explanatory. "Okay, I trust everyone completed today's reading assignment. Please make sure you bring something to take notes. You will be successful with your tests." At that point, people took out laptops and opened them. We were given instructions to not open our textbooks yet. "What is your definition of the word subconscious?" There was a brief pause after the question. Then slowly, several hands began to rise. "Well, I'm so glad to see the exuberance in this participation."

"Professor Roberts," I interjected, "I think that subconscious means when a person doesn't truly understand his or her potential."

"Very good. I don't know your names yet, and it will be a few more classes before I know."

"My name is Blythe Taylor."

"Blythe, you are on the right track." She then presented the definition and the word on the smart board. *Subconscious: of or concerning the part of the mind of which one is not fully aware, but which influences one's actions.*

Professor talked a little bit more before she released us for the day. I left the building and headed for the library. While walking, I thought more about that word 'subconscious.' I read that word in the textbook, but it hadn't settled with me until class time. In my mind, I began to apply this word to children being bullied in school. I was thinking that there were so many circumstances that went along with bullying, but according to the word 'subconscious,' a child lacked self-awareness and self-esteem. I was one of the blessed ones because I had my family support. I thought, 'If only children knew their potential and who they really are, that would help to disarm a lot of bullies.'

I decided to devote at least an hour to read for my Thursday class, plus possibly getting a head start on some of my paper projects. Before I realized, I was in the library for three hours. The time had really slipped by.

Leaving the library, I headed for the dorm to lie down. Upon my arrival, I flopped down on the bed. I lay there with the thoughts of how I could really help bullied children. I realized that children of all ages and grades were subject to bullying, but I wanted my focus to be on middle-school-aged children, preferably seventh-graders. Finally, I drifted off to sleep.

Mandy came into the room shortly after I was waking up. I was hungry, since I only had coffee for breakfast and nothing for lunch. We decided to eat dinner in the cafeteria, so we headed there.

We quickly ordered our dinner and just as quickly, we ate and departed. Once we reached the room, I thought about my feelings and what I learned in class today. "Mandy, I need to ask you a question."

"Shoot," she replied.

"Why are children bullied?"

"I think there are many reasons why children are bullied. I think that most bullying begins with verbal attacks. The victim usually has no self-esteem or the wherewithal to defend themselves. Then, that same concept can be the same for the perpetrator."

"What do you mean?" I asked.

"I mean," Mandy said, "the same way a victim doesn't realize his or her potential, the perpetrator doesn't have a clue to who he or she really is. Many bullies come off as being tough, but on the inside are really scared. Have you ever noticed that bullies never travel alone, that they usually have a following?"

"I guess I never looked at it like that, but that's exactly how it turned out with me," I said.

"Blythe, I'm not all that attractive to look at. My family doesn't have a lot of money, but I worked hard to go to college. I wasn't popular in school because of where I lived

59

and the type of clothes I wore. I played soccer in high school, and I worked hard to get here. My mom was very supportive, and the school district supplied me a mentor. I don't know where I would be if for not those two people.

"People, at first, left me alone. When I walked the halls, I would occasionally see people staring at me with a frown on their face, but no one said anything to me until Cindy started. Cindy was the captain of the cheerleading team and very popular. However, when Cindy began to single me out as her target, she had most of the cheerleading team to join in with her."

"Mandy, our past bullying experience seems almost identical. I had a mentor also. While I was going through the bullying incidents, I asked myself, 'What did I do to deserve this?' I also said, 'I did nothing to anyone.'

"I thought it was my fault that my parents broke up and gave me up for adoption. I internalized everything at first, but just like you, my mom was there to walk me through the difficult times. Then later, my mentor helped me by mainly listening to me. She taught me that it wasn't a good thing to keep everything inside but to talk about it with a special someone. Then, I had a special friend named Cara who was always there no matter what."

"Melissa was my special friend in middle school," Mandy interjected.

"Mandy, I've really been thinking about this word 'subconscious' since I left class today. We discussed this word in class and I believe it plays a key part in what we're talking about, in bullied victims and the perpetrator as well. In my philosophy class today, Professor Roberts asked what our definition of the word 'subconscious' was, and I said that subconscious means when a person doesn't truly understand his or her potential."

"I don't get it, Blythe," Mandy said.

"Don't you see? I said the bully really has no clue who they really are. They have no real identity and are unsure of what and who they really can be, so he or she assumes this make-believe person who people can easily accept.

"With this false identity, it is so easy to pick on those who seem helpless in defending themselves or choose not to fight back. I believe that bullies are just as afraid on the inside."

"Sounds like you've become an advocate for the bully," Mandy snapped back.

"No, not at all. Bullying is wrong on any level. School is supposed to be about learning academically and socially. Bullying deprives one of these things along with taking away one's dignity and self-respect. To sum it all up, bullies themselves are really scared, and that's why they get someone to follow them. Then, they pick on someone who seems weaker than they are."

"So, how do we stop bullying?" Mandy asked.

"I don't know about stopping it, but I have an idea to give it a knuckle sandwich.

"I want to become a mentor in a middle-school setting. I believe one strategy to help disarm a bully would be to teach the victims about self-esteem. Later on, I want to meet with bullies themselves. I don't know what to say, but when the time comes, I will certainly know."

"Sounds like a great plan," Mandy replied.

"I'm going to see my advisor tomorrow and ask if there's any way I can volunteer a few hours in a local school."

Wednesday morning was here. I was excited because I had found my purpose, and that was to give back to someone that walked in my former shoes. I hurriedly got dressed. Then Mandy and I quickly headed for the cafeteria. I fixed myself a cup of coffee. Then I had cereal and a bagel with cream cheese. Mandy ordered the same thing.

We were up talking so late last night, and we overslept this morning. It was 7:30 already. Time sure went by fast. We ate in a hurry, said our goodbyes, and headed for our classes. I was awakened with such great joy in my soul. I was excited because potentially there was a child waiting for me to help them. I would go to my advisor's office and talk with her immediately after class.

Psychology class went by very quickly. I headed over to my advisor's office in Kessler Hall. I made it there in five minutes. I opened the single glass front door and walked down a long corridor. Immediately, I came to a set of glass double doors. I went through them, and the first office to my right was my advisor's office. I came to a long gray counter and a young lady standing on the other side. "May I help you?" she said.

"Yes, I would like to see my advisor, Mrs. Alveary," I replied.

"Your name please."

"Blythe Taylor," I responded. She informed me that my advisor had someone in her office and she would tell her I was waiting to see her.

No sooner than I took a seat, Mrs. Alveary called my name and came out to greet me. She escorted me to her office and pointed to where I may sit. Then she went around this short bluish-gray desk and took her seat. Her desk was covered with files and papers of all kinds. She peered over her rectangular-shaped glasses and asked me, "Well, Blythe, what can I do for you?"

I was unsure if she remembered my name. "I have a request. First, allow me to say something. I was a victim of bullying while attending middle school.

"As much as I loved school, I began to develop a loathing for school. I fought hard to maintain good grades, and it was just as hard to make the cheerleading squad, but when someone plastered all over social media that I was adopted and I wasn't wanted in her school any longer, none of those things mattered to me anymore.

"This person talked about my freckles and made statements that I was too fat to be a cheerleader. I was devastated to no end. It was the love of my family that pulled me through, and I had a wonderful mentor who listened to me, and that is what I want to become, a mentor to a child that is suffering the same plight as I have."

"Well, young lady, that is an unusual request indeed. However, it is against school policy for freshmen to do any clinicals of any sort. Here at Winston State, we feel that it would be best for juniors to begin any clinicals to go alongside their three-hundred-level courses."

"Miss Alveary, I'm taking philosophy-110 this semester. Yesterday, we studied the word 'subconscious,' and the definition of that word applies to me, and it applies to every bullied victim and the perpetrator as well. Bullied people have lost their identity through the lack of self-worth and self-esteem.

"In turn, the perpetrator usually takes his lack of self-worth and self-esteem out on someone who seems beneath himself."

"It seems like you have stumbled upon something, but I don't—"

"Miss Alveary, this means so much to me. I am really beginning to discover who I really am.

"My biological mother named me something with meaning because it means carefree. However, my life has been anything but carefree. I really understand now that things will happen in my life, but I don't have to let them get me down. All I'm asking is for an opportunity to help some child understand their potential and value."

"Blythe, I'm convinced, but there still stands that rule against freshmen engaging in any clinical activities. However, I want you give me a brief report on what you want to do and why. Bring that back to me so I can present it to the Teacher Education Board. I can't promise you anything though."

"Okay, I will have it to you tomorrow. Thank you so much, Miss Alveary."

"You're welcome, Blythe."

While walking back to the dorm building, expectation and excitement had filled my soul, and it felt as if I was walking on air. I know that my request could go either way, but I chose to believe that everything will work in my favor. I don't know if it was due to this great feeling that now overwhelmed me, but I was standing in front of my dorm building. I rushed upstairs and cried out, "Mandy!" Mandy was sitting at her desk, reading. She quickly turned around to look at me. "Guess what? I went to see Miss Alveary, my advisor, a few minutes ago. I asked about becoming a mentor in a middle school. First, she told me that freshmen couldn't engage in any clinical activities, but when I persevered, she told me write down a brief statement explaining what and why I want to do."

"I'm so excited for you, roomie. I know that you will make a wonderful mentor."

"Thanks, Mandy," I replied. I pulled out my laptop, sat down at my desk, and began to tap on the keys. I gave a brief history of what I had gone through in middle school and the devastating things bullying had done to me, and if not for the love and support of my family and a very special lady who mentored me, I didn't think I would be here. Further, I stated that I wanted to mentor a child or children. Finally, I stated this program won't affect my grades in a negative way. I signed my name and printed out the document.

The morning came, with me waking up around 8:00. Apparently, Mandy had already left because there was no sign of her in the room. I quickly showered, got dressed, and headed downstairs for coffee only because there was too much excitement on my part to eat. Before I reached the cafeteria, I briefly stopped on the way and checked my folder to make sure I had the letter I needed for Miss Alveary, and yes, there it was.

I entered the cafeteria, filled a to-go cup with coffee, and then headed out the door. I arrived at Miss Alveary's office in no time at all. I asked the young man if Miss Alveary was in. He responded by saying that she hadn't arrived yet, but she was expected in at any moment. "May I ask your name please?" he asked me while opening a book on the counter.

"My name is Blythe Taylor." He flipped through several pages and then flipped back.

With a concerned look on his face, he said, "I'm sorry but I don't see your name on her schedule, and she isn't accepting any walk-in appointments today."

"Oh, you don't understand. I'm just here to give her a paper. I'm not going to stay any length of time," I said.

"Oh, I see. You may leave the letter with me and I will ensure that she will receive it," said the young man.

"I appreciate that, but if it's all the same, I would like to give it to her personally. I will wait for her, but thank you anyway," I said.

"Well, have it your way," was his response as he sat at the desk on the other side of the counter.

I took out my cellphone and my headphones and began listening to music. Shortly thereafter, Miss Alveary came through the door carrying a large black bag. The young man greeted her first with an exuberant good morning, to which she replied in kind.

"Miss Alveary, this young lady is here to see you. I informed her that your schedule is way too busy to accept any walk-ins today."

"It's okay, Charles. I've been expecting her." Charles had such a look of disgust on his face as he narrowly peered in my direction. I'm so glad there wasn't any sun behind this look because it would have burned a hole in me. "Blythe, you're certainly bright-eyed this morning. Do you have the letter?"

"Yes, I have the letter, Miss Alveary," I said as I handed her the large manila envelope with excitement. "The TEB will meet this coming Monday, so I will have an answer for you no later than Tuesday. What time is your class on Tuesday?" she asked.

"Ten-thirty until twelve-thirty," I responded.

"When you get out of class, come right over to my office, and we can do without scheduling an appointment. How does this sound to you?"

"Sounds great to me and thank you, Miss Alveary."

"You're welcome, Blythe. I will see you on Tuesday. Have a great time for the rest of your day."

"You as well, ma'am. Goodbye." I left the room feeling nervous about the looming decision, but at the same time hopeful of having my request granted. I scurried over to my philosophy class. Today consisted of instruction and a lot of note-taking. Professor Roberts told that our first quiz will come on Tuesday, and it will cover chapters one and two. Then after the quiz, we will cover Chapter Three in class. Finally, she stated our first paper was due on the third week of class, before midnight Thursday.

Things seemed to tighten a little, but if I used my time wisely. I would accomplish this by utilizing my time before, between, and after classes to read, study, and do my research. Fortunately, this first paper will only be one-page, APA style, with at least one supportive source. We must choose between being a traditionalist or non-traditionalist, as it pertained to the American educational system. In other words, did we believe in the status quo of the educational system or did we view it as oppressive and subjective and antiquated in its beliefs?

After class, I walked over to the cafeteria. I grabbed a quick lunch and then headed to my dorm. Once in my room, I immediately took out my laptop and sat at my desk. I took a deep breath while placing both hands on my head. Today's terms and definitions covered these two words, so I looked at them. I observed the non-traditionalist and its definition first and then the traditionalist view. As it pertains to education, non-traditionalists refuse to follow a set curriculum because they see it as oppressive and subjective. They feel their students will benefit more through their knowledge of the educational and political system. While there is some truth to this, the question is: how does one apply the necessary academics?

On the other hand, a traditionalist holds to view maintaining traditional values of a set curriculum as opposed to change. I had never been the upset-the–apple-cart type. I believed that one must work within the system to bring about change, and in this case, the educational system, after pondering a few minutes more, I began typing my paper. The thoughts were coming so fast that my fingers seemingly couldn't keep up on the keyboard.

The next thing I realized was that my paper was finished. Now, all I had to do was cite my source. Once I completed that, I saved my paper and began reading Chapter Three of my philosophy book.

Mandy soon came in. Evidently, she was exhausted because she vehemently dropped her book bag on the floor and dropped hard down on her bed. She lay there silently for a moment and then said, "Hey, roomie, how was your day?"

"My day was good. How was yours?"

"Mine was long. I have some reading to do for tomorrow's economic class," Mandy said.

"I just finished writing my first philosophy paper, and since I want to mentor bullied children, I had to turn in a special request to my advisor.

"Evidently there is a rule against freshmen doing any clinicals, so she will represent me before the Teacher Education Board on Monday."

"Blythe, I'm sure everything will go well for you. I think it's a great thing that you desire to help young people. I don't think there's anyone who could do it better. Maybe later I could join you."

"That would be great, Mandy. We could be the dynamic duo against bullying." I glanced over at Mandy with a huge smile. "Thanks Mandy."

"For what?"

"Just thanks."

Mandy took out a pad with what looked like notes on it, along with a textbook entitled *Understanding Economics*. I took out my 'math for teachers' workbook and briefly glanced through it. We studied until dinnertime. Then we headed out to get something to eat. After returning from the cafeteria, we mutually decided to go to the lounge on our floor and watch television. There were only a few other girls in the lounge, and they seemingly were oblivious to the television because they were engaged in a heavy conversation. Since I wasn't a big television person, Mandy was delegated to choose a good program. Mandy took the remote from the stand and began surfing through the channel guide. After a few moments, we settled for a movie we both liked.

The guide said the movie would last for one hour and forty-five minutes. However, the movie was watching both of us more than we were watching it. I kept fidgeting to keep awake, and Mandy was sound asleep. With the movie yet playing, I decided it was time for bed. As I arose from the chair, I called out to Mandy to tell her I was going to bed. Mandy stumbled to her feet, turned off the television, and we headed for our room.

It was Friday morning, and I survived the first week of class. I was feeling good about the things I had accomplished. I had one of my first papers written, I was working on becoming a mentor, and this was my final class for the week. Class wasn't until three o'clock, so I was going to spend as much time as possible in reading and studying. Mandy had already left for class, like previous mornings.

Class time quickly approached, so I gathered all my necessary things and left the dorm building. This class, unlike my other two, was quite a distance away. Therefore, I had to give myself a little more time to get there. Upon my arrival, I observed this large, brightly colored classroom with four rows of long tables with brown-colored tops. I counted nine chairs at each table. The chairs were nearly full, except for three seats. I occupied one of the three remaining seats. There were backpacks on the floor and laptops open and ready to go. Unlike my other two classes, whereas we brought a hard copy of the syllabus, this professor had uploaded it on the school's website. There was low-lying chatter coming from some of the students, while some were busy reading textbooks from other classes. Suddenly, a high-pitched voice cut through the chatter, causing the chatter to cease, and those reading looked up in the voice's direction.

"We will get started in five minutes. There are supposed to be thirty-two students enrolled in this class, so I want to give them a chance to get here." While he was speaking, the last two students hurriedly came in and quickly sat down.

"Well, looks like everyone is here. Good afternoon. My name is Professor Jansen, and welcome to 'math for teachers-1.' By a show of hands, how many of you have already looked at the syllabus for this class?" Since I was seated in the last row, I had a visual of the entire classroom, and every student responded by raising a hand.

"Great! This course is not about algebra, calculus, trigonometry, or any such thing. This course is designed to teach you how you will teach your students different algorithms in addition, subtraction, multiplication, and division. There will be five major tests given this semester; one will be your mid-term, and one will be the final exam."

"There will also be pop quizzes, and that means unannounced, so as long as you do well on your homework assignments, you should be okay. Are there any questions?" There was no response. "Okay, let's begin by introducing ourselves. Oh, I forgot. Please forgive me. This is 'math for teachers-1.' There will be a 'math for teachers-2' that you must take in order to graduate. There is also an algebra course that you must take in order to round out your math requirements. Okay, let's begin the introductions with the back table." I was seated at the end of the last table, so I was the first to go. The introductions didn't take long, and at the end, he began his lecture on Chapter One which covered the base ten system. He concluded his lecture with ten minutes of class time left. "That's all for today, and there will be no homework assignment, so you're dismissed."

While putting my things away, a moderately handsome young man came over and began talking to me. "Hi, my name is Todd, and what's your name? You must forgive me, but I'm terrible with names at first."

"That's okay. My name is Blythe," I responded.

"That's a name one doesn't hear every day, but it's an interesting name. What do you think of the class?"

"I like it a lot. I love math, so I think I will do well."

"I believe that too, Blythe." As we went through the doors to go outside, he said, "Oh, there's a small group of us meeting at DeVecchio's Pizza at six. Do you want to come?" I hesitated for a slight moment. Todd said, "Don't worry. It will be guys and girls going."

Thoughts quickly raced through my mind. In my mind, I thought to ask Mandy to come along also. "Okay, my roommate and I will come, so see you there at six."

"Okay, see you then," Todd said.

When I arrived at home, Mandy was lying on her bed with her ear buds in both ears. Once again, the music was loud enough to where I could hear it. Twice I called her name, and on the second call, she rose up on her bed and snatched out the earphones. "Girl, you scared me. What's going on?"

"Are you hungry, Mandy?"

"Yeah, I haven't eaten yet," she replied.

"Good. I met this nice guy in class, and he invited me out for pizza with a group of his friends. I told him that I would bring my roommate too."

"I don't know, Blythe. I'm not one to join in with people. My God, girl, you don't know this guy or his friends. He could be a nut, an undercover stalker, or anything. He might even be a serial killer," she said as she raised a pen in a stabbing motion. We both broke out in laughter.

"Girl, get serious! It's not like we're going on a date. We're only going out to get pizza. Now come on!"

Healing at Devecchio's

When we arrive at the restaurant, I see Todd seated with two young men and three young women. There were two tables together. Mandy and I approached the tables. Todd saw us and immediately stood up. He came around and pulled out our chairs, asking us to be seated. Once he regained his seat, he said, "Everyone, this is Blythe. We met in class today, and I invited her to join us for pizza. This is her roommate, uh…"

"Her name is Mandy," I interjected.

"Blythe, Mandy, this is Sophie, Janet, and Brian." They all waved simultaneously and spoke. Janet and Brian greeted us with a smile, but Sophie gave out a half smile and quickly turned her head away. Mandy and I, for some reason, both caught on and smiled at each other. Todd beckoned me to be seated next to him, with Sophie on the other side.

"Well, Blythe, what are you studying to become?" Sophie asked.

"I'm studying to become a teacher," I replied.

"A teacher, well, that sounds kind of boring."

"Cool it, Sophie. We only came to have a good time," Todd said.

"And I plan to have a good time, Todd. I'm just getting acquainted with your friend Blythe. Blythe, what kind of name is that? Is it German, East-European, or what?"

"I'm not quite sure, but my mom says it means 'carefree.'"

"Carefree, I wish life was carefree because my life has been anything but carefree. Let me tell you something, miss high and mighty. I'm here on financial aid. I will have to get a job to have some extra money in my pocket. My dad walked out on us and left us broke. My mom had to struggle to make ends meet, and I was bullied in school for not living in an upper-class neighborhood, or not wearing the right clothing.

"Kids said my name sounded like a couch you sit on. I was talked about and ridiculed beyond belief."

"Sophie, I feel your pain because I was bullied in middle school as well. I was ridiculed and even had my personal business exposed on social media." I asked everyone at our table a question. "How many of you were bullied in some fashion?" Every hand was raised. "In my philosophy class, we read about the word 'subconscious.'

"This word simply means that one has not discovered his or her true self. Many times, we allow the things we've gone through to define us, and that's what happened to me. I was unsure of myself, and I constantly needed the approval of others to define me. Now, I know what I want and I'm going after it."

In contrast to before, Sophie was a lot calmer. "Blythe, guys, I'm sorry. I don't know what came over me. Blythe, please accept my apology." Everyone seemingly perked up, whereas previously their heads were lowered.

"It's okay. I want to help people that have gone through like us, and some are still in it. However, I believe that once a person comes to know themselves, nothing can stop them. My goal is helping both the victim and the perpetrator, hopefully to bring an end to bullying."

"Shouldn't the focus be on the victims and healing them?" Janet asked.

"Certainly, but bullies suffer from a lack of identity as well. I believe bullies on the inside are just as scared. My dear friend Mandy helped me to see that. She showed me that bullies often travel with a following because someone might retaliate against them. Also, bullies pick on someone weaker than themselves to make themselves look better," I said.

By the time I finished speaking, two large pizzas arrived at our table, and before we began to eat, Sophie was wiping tears from her eyes with a restaurant napkin as she said, "Thanks, Blythe. You are amazing, and you will make a great mentor."

"Thanks, Sophie. I just hope I don't fall flat on my face." The rest of the evening was filled with jubilant laughter and talking until we departed from the restaurant.

It was 9:00 p.m. when we left the restaurant. Mandy and I took our time returning to the dorm room. We walked a few blocks without a word spoken. I was reflecting on the entire evening, and I felt good. Mandy broke the silence. "Blythe, what you did tonight was really awesome. When

Sophie verbally attacked you, you handled the entire situation very professionally."

"While you were speaking, everyone at the table was paying attention to you despite all the noise surrounding us in that place. I guess what you said about that word 'subconscious' really came true for you. I know it became a reality to Sophie, and Blythe, from now on it is a reality to me. I'm going to put my best foot forward in all I do."

Mandy finished her last sentence as we approached the stairs. "Thanks, roomie. At first when she came at me, I could only visualize the girl who bullied me in junior high. I wanted to retaliate with anger as well, but something deep inside me allowed only understanding. I don't know. Maybe tonight was a testing period for me. I don't want to get the big head but—"

Mandy interjected, "That head of yours can't fit through the door right now." We both laughed and I threw my pillow at her, and she retaliated in kind.

We briefly laughed and playfully taunted each other for a few more moments. "Mandy, I'm going to hit the shower tonight and then try to get a little reading done. That's if the little sleeping-reading fairy doesn't show up and sprinkle fairy dust in my eyes," I said with a chuckle.

"Girl, that's the fairy from Peter Pan." Mandy was laughing uncontrollably.

Immediately after my shower, my mom called, and she had the rest of our family there too. I pushed the little green video button so we could talk and see each other. They were checking to see how my first week went. And I gave them the full rundown of this week's events, including what took place tonight. I also told them that I wanted to become a mentor in a local school for bullied victims.

My mom and dad thought this was a great idea. The conversation didn't last very long because I told them I needed to read some before going to sleep. Mandy told them to have a good night, and they wished us both the same.

The weekend quickly ended, in direct contrast to how the first week of school passed. Monday morning was here in full bloom because I was anticipating my advisor acting on my behalf before the TEB. I completed today's required reading over the weekend. Class consisted of a discussion on the reading assignment.

After class, I grabbed a bite to eat and then headed to the library to start my research for a paper that would be due very soon. I lost track of time because I went into the library at 2:30 p.m. and now it was 6:30 p.m. I was mentally exhausted, and I needed a light snack, a hot shower, and then bed.

Tuesday morning came, and I had a torrent of high expectations, for today was the day that Miss Alveary said that she would be in contact with me concerning my mentoring. I quickly leaped out of bed, got dressed, and ran down to the cafeteria for breakfast.

Breakfast usually wasn't a big deal for me. However, I was feeling on top of the world, so why not splurge? In previous mornings, I just passed by the Danish pastries and headed toward the coffee, but today was different.

As soon as I gathered my breakfast and took my seat, my phone rang. The screen said: *Winston State University*, but I was certain this was the call from Miss Alveary. "Hello," I said.

"Blythe, this is Miss Alveary. How are you this morning?"

"Great, and how are you?"

"Fine. Listen, I have your answer from the board. Is it possible for you to come see me today?" At that moment, all the sprightliness in me began to quickly evaporate.

"Yes, ma'am. I can be there in a few minutes. Is that okay?"

"Yes, Blythe, that will be fine. I will see you in a few minutes. Bye."

"Bye, Miss Alveary."

I desperately wanted to ask her what the decision was, but if she wanted me to know, she would have said. Then, some thoughts and questions began to arise, thoughts and questions such as: why didn't she give me the results now? Why do I have to go to her office? Then, the voice of reasoning began to speak in the form of: maybe she doesn't like giving bad news over the phone.

At this point, I felt as if there was a good angel on one shoulder and an evil angel on the other one. After a moment, I told myself, 'No matter the outcome of the report, it will all be fine. If I can't mentor now, then maybe it wasn't meant to be, and a time will surely come.'

I arrived at her office, and she was standing at the huge brown desk. She escorted me to her office and gestured for me to have a seat. I followed her directions and took a seat. She went around her desk and sat down. "Blythe, as I said to you over the phone, I have your answer from the board. I know you're probably wondering why I had you come here and simply not give you the answer when we talked previously. Well, they have given you special permission to mentor a student at a middle school a few blocks from here.

"However, they want a detailed report before the end of this semester, turned into me, and you must start with only one day a week. You must go to the school and meet the principal, and she will choose the child for you. We already have a standing relationship with Murray Middle School because that's where we send our students when it's time for their novice and student teaching."

"When you asked me to come here, I thought the answer would be 'no.' I had a lot of thoughts and questions running through my mind."

"Whatever made you think that, Blythe? No dear, I had to lie down the expectations of your request. Now Blythe, are there any questions?"

"Yes, when can I start?"

"What is the best day for you, dear?"

"Will this Friday be okay?"

"Blythe, as long as that works for you. I will notify the school and tell them you will be there on Friday."

Time had rapidly gone by. I glanced at the clock, and it showed I had only ten minutes to get to class.

"Miss Alveary, thank you so much, but I only have ten minutes to get to class on time. Thank you again."

"You're welcome, Blythe. You better skedaddle."

I left her office feeling on Cloud Nine. I began to think that I was going to make a difference in some young person's life. I thought about one day starting my own mentoring and anti-bullying center, but for now, I would settle with mentoring whatever student was assigned to me.

I breezed through class, and soon I was on my way back to the dorm. I couldn't wait to tell Mandy when she got in. I texted my mom at work and told her the great news. In a few moments, she replied with, *"That's wonderful, sweetheart. Call me later. I love you."* I wanted to eat because I'm famished, but Mandy would be home in an hour, and hopefully we could eat together.

When Mandy entered the room, I began to literally jump up and down with excitement. "Mandy, are you hungry?"

"No, I ate something earlier. Are you hungry?"

"Yes, but I have something great to tell you. Come with me while I eat, and I'll tell you about it, okay?"

When we got to the cafeteria, I put a plethora of food on my tray. I had my entrée of chicken strips, a garden salad, some watermelon, and finally, a big delectable slice of double chocolate layer cake. I couldn't recall ever eating this much food at one time. Mandy only wanted something to drink, so she grabbed us both a soft drink, and we met at the table.

After we were seated, I began to pour out to Mandy about today's meeting with Miss Alveary. "I am really excited, Mandy. I mean I feel like life really has a purpose now."

"Girl, you really must be excited. Look at all the food you have there. I have never seen you eat this much before." We both laughed.

"Blythe, I know you're excited and all, but may I caution you about something?"

"Certainly."

"I believe that one day this will all pay off what you're about to do, but this will not be an easy task. I mean, people will always be people. I'm not saying you can't or won't make a difference, but really know what you will be up against. Do you understand what I'm trying to say?"

"Yes, I hear you loud and clear. You know, I have a dear friend back home named Cara. While I was going through the bullying, she was the only true friend who stayed with me through it all. I valued her opinion and I value yours. It's as if God has been watching over me through everything by placing the right people in my life."

"Blythe, you're going to make me cry with all this soft stuff, and I'm supposed to be a hard-nosed soccer player. I can't be seen blubbering at this table. I will say one thing though. You are a very special person, and I'm glad we're roomies. Now, enough of this soft mushy stuff." We both laughed hysterically as we began to leave.

We continued to talk as we traveled to the dorm, and briefly in the room. By the time night came, I was mentally exhausted. However, physically I was ready to take on anything. I guessed the mental exhaustion took over because by bedtime, I went to sleep seemingly without hesitation.

The Next Friday

It appeared the second week of classes took forever to pass. However, today would be the day when I could begin my mentoring at a local middle school. Miss Alveary called me on Thursday to inform me on where to go, and my contact person.

She said the name of the school was Holly Branch Middle School, and its location was within walking distance from the university. It was located on Bloom Street, which was behind the library. My contact person was the principal Mr. Edwards. Miss Alveary also informed me that Mr. Edwards would designate the proper child when I meet him.

Miss Alveary gave me the phone number to call the school to set an appointment with the principal. It was still early, and not knowing what time Mr. Edwards arrived, I played it safe and waited until nine o'clock to call. This would also allow things to settle down because if it was anything like my old middle school, with students getting off buses and parents dropping off some, things got quite hectic at morning time.

Nine o'clock soon rolled around, and I was dialing the number without hesitation. After three rings, a pleasant and calming voice answered. "Thank you for calling Holly Branch Middle School, where great things are happening. How might I help you?"

"My name is Blythe Taylor, and I'm a student at Winston State. I have been approved to become a mentor of a student there, but today I need to set an appointment with Mr. Edwards."

"Hold please." After a momentary pause, a deep male voice said, "Hello, Mr. Edwards speaking."

"Hello, Mr. Edwards. This is Blythe Taylor, and my advisor, Miss Alveary, said you would be expecting a call from me concerning mentoring of a child."

"Oh yes, Blythe. Is it possible to meet with me at 11:00 this morning? That way you can meet the child, and we can discuss the parameters."

"Yes, sir. I will be there at 11:00."

"See you then, Blythe."

"Goodbye, sir."

I had forty-five minutes before I would meet with Mr. Edwards, so I took a seat under a large shade tree, took out my cellphone and headphones, and listened to music. Before I realized, I only had ten minutes before my meeting. I scrambled to my feet and began walking toward the library. As I approached the library, I went to the south side of the building, and there was a small parking lot. Directly behind the small parking lot sat Orchard Street. On the other side of the street, there was an aggregation of houses that belonged to the university.

To my left, there was Billing's Science Hall. I continued to my right on Orchard Street, walked down three blocks, and I saw a mundane school building. The school had a mediocre parking lot which one must access from Orchard Street. There was a lane that was specifically meant for buses. There was a backdoor with a sign that said: *"All visitors must use the front door."*

As I walked toward the front of the building, I bypass a side door that sat on Kilpatrick Avenue. I turned left on Bloom Street, walked a few more feet, and came upon double doors. One of the doors had a sign which said: *"ALL VISITORS MUST REPORT TO THE OFFICE."* I looked down to my left. Mounted on the wall was a gray box with a button and a speaker.

There weren't any instructions, so I pushed the small gray button. I heard the sound that was equivalent to a phone ringing. After a few rings, a woman's voice said, "May I help you?"

"Yes, my name is Blythe Taylor, and I have a meeting with Mr. Edwards." After a slight hesitation, a buzzing sound came from the door as the voice simultaneously said, "Left door please." I grasped the left door handle, pulled the door toward me, and proceeded inside. Once inside, this short hallway only led to the office. I guessed with all the school shootings in our country, security must have priority. I went up to a long brown counter. I thought to myself while I chuckled inside, 'There must be a market for these kinds of counters.'

"How may I help you?" said a woman with a different-sounding voice than the one on the speaker. However, she was the only person in the office at the time. "My name is Blythe Taylor, and I have an eleven o'clock appointment with Mr. Edwards." The lady sauntered away from her desk, walked down a brief hall, and disappeared into a room near her desk.

Moments later, a tall, slender man with blond hair came to the counter. "Blythe Taylor, my name is Phil Edwards. It's so wonderful to meet you," he said as he extended his hand.

I extended my hand to meet his in a joyous handshake. "It's nice to meet you as well, Mr. Edwards," I said with enthusiasm.

"Well, if you will come this way, we can talk in my office."

"Yes, sir," I replied. I stepped to my right around the end of the counter, and after about ten steps, we were at his office.

"You may be seated here," he said while gesturing to one of the two plush, red chairs. "Now tell me a little bit about yourself."

"Well, sir, my name is Blythe Taylor, and I'm a freshman at the university. What else would you like to know, sir?"

"I would like to know what compelled you to become a mentor for a bullied child?"

"Mr. Edwards, my main goal is to give back in the form of helping to instill self-esteem in those that are or have been bullied. I was bullied in middle school. I was teased about my freckles, my height, even my being in foster care, and having bi-racial parents. You see, sir, I was given up for adoption at the age of four.

"I have even had my adoption business put on social media. I know how devastating it is to be treated as an outcast and to feel devastated to the point of giving up. Mr. Edwards, a bullied person lacks self-esteem and really has no identity. I believe if a bullied person can somehow begin to tap into who he or she really is, they will be changed forever.

"Sir, I am studying the word 'subconscious' in my philosophy class. I believe that word is associated with one not realizing their potential, and I want to help a child or children see their potential."

"Interesting concept, Blythe. Okay. School times begin at 8:30 and end at 3:30. Jada, the child I have designated for you, is in seventh grade. What day and time are you available?"

"I have classes on Monday and Wednesday from 8:30 until 10:30, Tuesday and Thursday from 10:30 until 12:30, and Friday from 3:00 until 5:00."

"Blythe, according to your schedule and Jada's lunchtime, the two of you can meet on Mondays, Wednesdays, and Fridays at 11:00. How does that sound?"

"Sounds great to me, sir."

"Okay, so if you come in on Monday, I can introduce you two."

"Have a great weekend, Mr. Edwards, and thank you."

"You have a great weekend as well, Blythe, and see you on Monday at eleven."

I returned to the dorm room and flopped down on the bed. I began to reflect on today's events, and before I knew it, I was asleep.

As I woke up, I picked up my phone to check the time. The screen read: *2:30.* I scrambled out of bed once again, brushed my hair and my teeth, and then headed off to math class.

Meeting Jada

The weekend rapidly vaporized, and Monday had arrived. I began to prepare to meet Jada, almost like one would prepare for job interview. I wanted everything to be right. I needed every hair to be in place, so I brushed with extra fervency. I chose my best skirt and blouse and matching shoes. I was always taught that one's first impression is the best impression, so I must look my best. I never looked bad, but this was not a blue jeans kind of day.

I headed off to class, and when I arrived, I was met with glaring eyes from some of my classmates. I was not one to wear high heels, so I felt sort of awkward. I made my way to my seat, and as soon as I was seated, a classmate named Ken leaned over and whispered, "Blythe, what's up? You look very nice. I mean, you always look nice in a blue jeans kind of way, but today you really look nice."

"I have someone to meet after class, no biggie though."

Ken eased himself erect in his seat with a puzzled look on his face. I chuckled to myself while I prepared for class. Class ended precisely at 10:30. I gathered my belongings and headed off to Holly Branch. I had plenty of time, so I took my time in walking. I arrived at the school at 10:45, got buzzed in, told the secretary why I was there, and took a seat.

While waiting on Mr. Edwards, I heard a voice over the loudspeaker say, "Will Jada Davis please report to the office?" By the conclusion of the transmission, Mr. Edwards emerged from his office, and almost simultaneously, a young girl quietly entered the office and stood in front of the counter. "Good morning, Miss Taylor, and good morning, Jada."

We both replied by saying, "Good morning, sir."

"Miss Taylor, this is Jada Davis, and Jada, this is Miss Taylor. Miss Taylor is a student at the university located down the street. She is volunteering to help a student, and we thought this would be a good thing for you. Kind of like a big sister. How does that sound, Jada?"

Jada had her head bowed down. Then she slightly raised it and quickly lowered it again. Jada was African-American and about my height (give or take an inch or two). She had thick bifocal lenses inside dark-framed glasses. Her clothing looked like everyone else because of the school-uniform policy. She was carrying a lunchbox. "That sounds fine, Mr. Edwards," Jada hesitantly answered.

"Miss Taylor will meet with you on your lunch break three times a week, and if it's okay with Miss Taylor, you two can start today."

"That's fine, Mr. Edwards," I responded.

"Okay, Jada, please show Miss Taylor to the cafeteria, and you two have a nice lunch."

We entered the cafeteria and I observed children seated around various tables, laughing and talking amongst themselves. I noticed that Jada sat down in an obscure table that had one other student, so I followed her and took a seat next to Jada.

"Miss Taylor, this is my friend Trina, and Trina this is Miss Taylor."

"Nice to meet you, Trina." I noticed that Trina was wearing a not-so-popular brand of shoes, and her hair looked uncombed. I looked around the cafeteria and observed the enjoyment on all the other children's faces while seemingly enjoying their break.

There were several staff redirecting the students into lowering the noise, to which they complied, only to increase the volume a moment later. "May I ask a question for either of you? Why do you two, and I see a few other tables with only a few students, sit by yourselves?"

Jada said, "We're not welcome at their tables." She pointed at the two rowdy tables. "Besides, we're both trying to stay as far away from some of them as possible. See that boy standing up that's wearing the short braids in his hair.

His name is Ronald Coleman, and he always starts trouble with Trina and me.

"He talks about us, calling us nerds, teachers' pet, and even though we have on a uniform, he still talks about our clothes. He talks about how thick my glasses are. One day, he said to me that he couldn't stand behind me if I faced the sun, for fear I might set him on fire. This is a constant thing."

I could see tears in Jada's eyes, and her bottom lip quivered slightly. Then Trina spoke out, "He even talks about how dark my skin is, and he's just as dark as I am. He only says these things when no staff is around.

"We have talked to our teachers, and they have told us to simply ignore. There is only so much ignoring we can do, and only so much we can take. Speaking for myself now, I tell my mom every day that I hate this school, and I don't want to be here."

It was only my intention to get to know Jada during our first visit, but as each of them communicated their stress, I could literally hear the frustration in their voices as well as see it in their faces.

I thought this would be a one-on-one situation, but it seemed this had presented itself as a match set. I guessed one must always be prepared to deal with any problem that presented itself. "Miss Jones," Jada asked, "why do some people have to be so mean? I mean, I can't help where I live, what clothes or shoes I wear, where my parents work, or anything else that some children pick to talk about."

"Yeah, I didn't ask for this life. I never asked to be born, and frankly, I'm sick and tired of it all," Trina said. Trina took this opportunity to empty her tray into the large gray trashcan that sat in the middle of the cafeteria.

As she proceeded, Jada told me, "Miss Jones, I have real trust issues, and I don't share my thoughts with many people, but I feel there's something genuine about you. There was one time when I thought about committing suicide because of how hopeless my situation seemed. Miss Jones, I felt I had no other way out.

"I don't know what stopped me, but those thoughts haven't gone away completely. I'm confused and I blame myself for allowing this happen to me."

Trina approached the table but heard the last sentence from Jada and nodded her head in agreement. "Jada, I thought our first meeting would be about us getting to know each other. Trina, you are an integral part of the group as well.

"I felt just as you two because I was bullied in middle school as well. I felt that everything was my fault, from having freckles to my biological parents putting me up for adoption. It took a long time for me to learn that absolutely none of it was my fault. And Jada, to answer your question, some children are mean because they don't really know themselves. Deep down, some of them are just as afraid as the person they bully.

"I think we are off to a great start because speaking out concerning what's bothering you hopefully made you feel better. It seems like the both of you harbored a great deal of resentment, but you have released a lot of it today. Last thing because there's only five minutes left of your lunchtime, I'm not here to offer my advice. I'm only here to listen and find out what you need and want."

"I do feel much better since we talked, Miss Jones," Jada said with a smile.

"I do too," Trina said.

"Ladies, I will see you again on Wednesday at eleven, and remember, I'm here for you. You are very special ladies, and no one can ever take that away from you, and remember that life isn't all about the outward things; it's about what you have inside of you."

The cafeteria monitor told the girls it was time to empty their trays because lunch was through for the day. The girls hastily walked away to join the other classmates, being extra careful to avoid the young man that was being totally obnoxious and loud. I thought to myself, 'I would relish the opportunity to find out what makes him tick. I would really like to test my own theory that bullies also can be reached if given the chance.'

Second Meeting

Classes were going well, and I must say my determination to maintain good grades seemed to be paying off because I was averaging an *A* in every one of my classes. I continued to devote my time outside of classes to reading, studying, and turning in every assignment on time. It was the day of my second meeting with Jada and Trina. I wasn't sure if it was okay for Trina to be included in our meetings, so I called Mr. Edwards and informed him of the situation with Trina. He said it was okay but cautioned me to not take on too much.

After class had concluded, I made my way to the school. Upon entering the cafeteria, I observed Ronald at the table where Jada and Trina sat, laughing hysterically and pointing at them. However, the young ladies weren't responding in kind, but they seemed unshaken no matter how much he laughed and pointed. The expression on their brightly gleaming faces was undaunted despite his raging tyranny. As I approached the table, he squinted out of the corner of one eye and quickly scampered away and continued his antics at his own table. "Good morning, ladies. I see Ronald is up to the same thing. Are you both okay? And how often does this behavior take place?"

"Pretty much every day. It used to really get to me, but ever since we met the other day, for some reason, it doesn't bother me as in the past. For the first time, I feel sorry for him," Jada said.

"Yeah, it's as if he's not happy himself, and he has to take his unhappiness out on us," Trina replied.

I was sitting there watching my vision unfold before my own eyes because of two reasons. These two girls were rapidly transforming into young ladies because they weren't sulking about their sorrows. Secondly, they were showing sympathy for the perpetrator. This was only our second meeting. I just felt that these young ladies needed someone to really listen to them and to give them an outlet to vent their frustration and anger.

The time quickly came to an end, and the ladies must return to class. They emptied their tray when the cafeteria monitor motioned for them to do so. However, this time they did something totally unexpected. Instead of avoiding the area where Ronald sat, they boldly walked through his barrage of verbal insults, smiling and keeping their heads high.

This way of exiting seemed to disarm Ronald because his tirade of laughter began to deteriorate with each contented step taken.

When I arrived in my dorm room, I called my mom to let her know how great things were going. "Hello," Mom answered.

"Hello, Mom. How is everyone?"

"Everyone is doing well. The question is: how are you? You must stay very busy, honey."

"I stay very busy, Mom, with studying, reading, and everything else. I am maintaining an *A* in each class."

"Outstanding, baby. I knew you had it in you. We are very proud of you."

"Thanks, Mom, but there's more."

I began to share the last two days' events with Jada and Trina, and how great it felt to be a part of their lives. We talked for over an hour, and our conversation concluded with Mom giving out cautions to me. Soon after, Mandy came in, and I knew I would be compelled to tell her.

The next few weeks went by very well. Each day, I would stop by the little bakery near the school and purchase three cookies, give one to Jada and one to Trina, and the three of us would laugh and talk. I could see a different look on their faces, in contrast to when we first met. There was a bright glow of surging confidence surrounding each of them. Evidently, Ronald noticed because his insults toward these two ladies began to become less and less.

His face now had a weird, puzzled look displayed on his face as his former victims strolled past him each day. It was as if his whole plan of attack had now become discombobulated. Then one day, something happened. As I was handing the two ladies their cookie, as had become our tradition, Ronald approached our table with a very serious look on his face. "Hey, lady, how come you bring cookies for them every day? I don't think that's fair."

"What is your name, young man?"

"Ronald Coleman," he replied.

"Well, Ronald Coleman, my name is Miss Taylor, and I bring cookies for my two special friends, and we would love for you to become a special friend as well. Wouldn't we, ladies?" They couldn't answer due to their mouths stuffed with their cookies, so they simply nodded their heads in agreement.

"I don't want a cookie, and I definitely don't want to sit over here with the nerds."

"I have a question, Ronald. Why would it be so terrible to sit over here with these beautiful young ladies?"

"I just can't. I have a reputation in this school."

"What type of reputation? There are both good and bad reputations, and they both have people following them.

"The question you must ask yourself is: how will you lead people? Will you show them a good example by helping others or a bad example through hurting others, and, Ronald, I believe you really want to help others. What do you say? I can see that you have the ability to lead others, so why not make a good choice and join us?"

Another lunch period came to an end. Ronald had a perplexed look on his face as he slowly turned and walked away. However, before he was totally out of my sight, he quickly spun around and speedily headed back in my direction. With a half grin on his round, plump face, he said, "Miss Jones, will you bring me a cookie next time?"

"Of course, but there's a catch. You must sit at our table to receive it. Deal?"

"Yes, ma'am. It's a deal."

When I arrived at the school for our next get-together, Ronald was seated at our table, just as he promised. However, he had placed some lengthy space between himself and the girls. "Good morning, everyone."

"Good morning, Miss Jones," the three replied.

"Let's do something new. Instead of you calling me Miss Jones, call me Blythe. How's that sound?"

The three all looked at one another with an inquisitive expression on their face, and suddenly Ronald became the self-appointed spokesperson. "Miss Jones, I mean, Blythe, I don't mean any disrespect, but I have never heard that name before."

"There's a story that goes with my name. My name means 'carefree,' but my life has been anything but carefree. I was bullied in middle school because of my name and because I'm adopted."

"You're adopted," Ronald chimed in.

"Yes, I'm adopted by a wonderful family. I have wonderful parents and a sister."

Jada said, "I have a little sister," while Trina said, "I have a little brother, and he's a nuisance."

"Just be thankful you have a little sister and brother." As I handed Ronald his cookie, I asked him, "Ronald, do you have siblings?" Ronald lowered his head to the table. "Ronald, what's wrong?" The child who was usually loud and boisterous was now silent. After a moment, Ronald slightly raised his head and broke his silence.

"Blythe, can I tell you something alone?"

"Sure, Ronald. Ladies, please excuse us," I said as we moved to another table, out of earshot.

"Blythe, no, I have no siblings. I'm in foster care too. I was taken out of my home because my mom's boyfriend drinks and fights my mom a lot, and he doesn't do anything to help my mom. My caseworker said he must leave our house, and until he does, I can't go back. While I was there, he constantly yelled at Mom and me." As he continued to talk, he gently lowered his head to try and conceal the giant tears falling from his tender face.

Ronald became more comfortable sitting with us. In fact, he asked three other young people to join us at lunchtime. Ronald became very close with Jada and Trina. In fact, when another child began to talk about my two young ladies, Ronald became the defender.

End of the First Year

By the end of my first year, everything was going smoothly. Jada, Trina, and Ronald were still very close. As a matter of fact, Ronald said his mother had completed everything the Child Services Agency had set down for her including finding great employment and another apartment, and Ronald soon would be home with her.

The young ladies were also showing a newness of life. They both came to school with new outfits and shoes and with their nails and hair done. They looked like they should belong on the cover of a modeling magazine.

Just to see the progress of these three young people brought exhilaration. Then, to cap it off, my personal goals were all fulfilled. I maintained an *A* average in all my classes, and I kept that average after completing my three final exams.

Since Holly Branch was out for the summer before my university, I had to say goodbye to all the children. Whereas I started with three, that number swelled greatly. The last day was filled with a litany of hugs and see-you in the fall. Jada, Trina, and yes, even Ronald were torn up because of our departure. I reminded them of their accomplishments that they achieved this school year and that they would be in the eighth grade in the fall.

I turned in report to Miss Alveary to show the progress of the children. I included that I was initially assigned to one student, but two other children were thrust upon me, and through no pre-determined selection of theirs nor mine.

My family came early to pick me up. I had everything packed up, and all that was left was to load into the car. Once this task was completed, Mandy and I exchanged our goodbyes and hugged each other. As I departed, I began to survey the now-empty room. I thought about all the great things which took place this school year, and I didn't have a care in the world.

The Next Three Years

I completed my sophomore, junior, and senior years with the same determination that I had as a freshman. The only difference was that my freshmen and sophomore years were spent getting my general education courses out of the way. Having successfully accomplished that, my junior and senior years were filled with my three-hundred-level courses, five teacher certification tests, novice teaching, and finally student teaching, and likewise, these tasks were appropriately completed.

I was able to see my children at Holly Branch again during their eighth-grade year, but after that, they were off to high school. During the next two years, I brought a voluminous number of cookies to our table in the cafeteria.

I accomplished my novice and student teaching during my senior year, and now all courses were complete. Mandy and I maintained a healthy bond as friends through all four years. Now here we stood together at graduation.

At the culmination of the ceremony, families were hugging, smiling, and rejoicing over their family members' success. I was so excited to see Cara there. I introduced her to Mandy, and they hit it off famously.

Our families took group pictures together. Then my sister, Cara, Mandy, and I took selfies and pictures with the four of us. My undergraduate life was now a thing of the past. Now, I was on to greater things.

Life Now

I had become the seventh-grade resource teacher at Rolland Middle School. It was my job to assist teachers with difficult students who were experiencing a lack in reading and writing skills. I had found out that some children learned better in a smaller learning environment. I still dealt with both the perpetrator and the victim of bullying at school with success. I had also started my own mentoring program outside of school called DAB, which stood for *Disarm a Bully*.

Summary

Blythe Taylor had to overcome insurmountable obstacles, such as being given up to adoption at the age of four and never knowing her biological parents. Although she was chosen by a wonderful family, that wasn't enough to cease her persecution because of her name. When she came to her wits' end and she decided to give up, her mother reminded her that Blythe meant 'carefree.'

CPSIA information can be obtained
at www.ICGtesting.com
Printed in the USA
LVHW050027100221
678896LV00007B/832

9 781643 785882